NORFOLK BROADS
The Golden Years

Pictures and Memories 1920s–1950s

by
Philippa Miller

Edited by

Peter Haining

HALSGROVE

First published in Great Britain in 2008

British Library Cataloguing-in-Publication Data
A CIP record for this title is available from the British Library

ISBN 978 1 84114 702 4

HALSGROVE

Halsgrove House
Rylenads Industrial Estate
Bagley Road, Wellington
Somerset TA21 9PZ
T: 01823 653777
F: 01823 216796
Email: sales@halsgrove.com
Website: www.halsgrove.com

DEDICATION

To the Memory of Peter Haining

1940–2007

Frontispiece photograph: *The 35-metre high
Longships lighthouse was built in 1875.*

Printed and bound in Great Britain by CPI Antony Rowe Ltd, Wiltshire

Broadland Memories
by *Philippa R. Miller*

Broadland...

Liquid Light
And a mirrored sky,
Cool green depths
As a boat glides by...

1935

Broadland Days

Dewdrops, daylight, dawn.
Stillness, sunrise, song.
Chatter, clouds and corn.
Willows, wind and waves.
Racing, ropes and reeds.
Merriment, meanderings.

Sails stowed up at sunset.
Ripples, rest, reflection.
Moonlight, mirages, mist.
Lamplight, lazy laughter.
Silver, silence, stars.
Peace, perfect peace.

1940s

'Busy Brundall' – a watercolour by Philippa Miller, c.1935.

The original photograph that inspired Busy Brundall.

Broadland: A Watery Paradise

The Norfolk Broads are a unique, watery paradise visited each year by thousands of people from towns and cities all over the British Isles; some even from other, far-flung, countries of the world. Yet a century ago they were hardly known, sparsely populated and almost untouched by the passage of time.

The rivers of East Anglia flow from north-west and south-east towards the East Coast, pouring their waters eventually into the North Sea through Great Yarmouth or Lowestoft. Hundreds of years ago, when these rivers were much wider, they flooded peat diggings to become the Broads as we know them today. Well-sited windmills – or, more correctly, wind pumps – were built to pump the water from the flooded marshes that later became good grazing grounds for cattle on their way to markets in London – some of them from as far away as Scotland.

Dawn at North Cove.

Today a few of these mills are still at work, while others are just picturesque landmarks on a flat, wild landscape.

Broadland, as it is often referred to, was very different and comparatively lonely during my childhood in the early years of the twentieth century. There was an abundance of wild flowers, the waters were crystal clear and the graceful designs of the few yachts and cruisers on the move added to the visual delights.

Even today Broadland is still an attractive playground – the more remote reaches and wide open Broads contrasting with the busy towns and centres. Coots and swans and an occasional heron are eager for titbits, while colourful ducks seem to be everywhere. The reeds swaying in the wind, the graceful willows bowing to the stream and an occasional sentinel windmill: all can enchant the eye. Alternatively, a happy party of visitors passing in their cruiser or a yachtsman busy tacking in a head wind contribute to days full of interest.

The quiet, lonely places bring pleasure and peace to those who take the trouble to seek them out. The wind rustling the reeds, a gentle 'plop' that can break the silence as a moorhen starts out on her swim or else a little nibbling sound which draws attention to a water rat having his breakfast or supper.

In earlier times, though, the traveller could watch the swaying weeds below the surface and perhaps

Left: *Majestic Thurne Mill.*

Below: *Racing on Oulton Broad.*

Isolated How Hill Mill.

Yachts near Coldham Hall.

Wind on Rockland Broad.

One of the great black-sailed wherries on the Broads, c.1910.

Reflections on Salhouse Broad.

'A Sail Beneath Haddiscoe Flyover' – a watercolour by Philippa Miller.

'The Beauties of Reedham' – a watercolour by Philippa Miller, c.1936.

'The Skipper' by Philippa Miller, 1930.

En route through the Broads.

The patient fisherman.

catch sight of a shoal of tiny fish as he drifted along in a little boat through a narrow dyke. It is a rare and thrilling moment now if you happen to see a kingfisher hesitate and make his lightning strike – returning to the same bough he left before swallowing the unlucky minnow he has caught.

Feeding a swan on Barton Broad.

Taking a ride!

Nestishead Dyke.

Houseboat for two – a perfect day on the Broads!

Above: *A coot at South Walsham.*

Left: *Punting along the Broads.*

There are still a few – a very few – places where the bittern can be heard or where a rare swallowtail butterfly wafts by. A line of willows bowing to their own reflections are often to be seen – but willow herb and meadowsweet are far less frequent for us to enjoy. Waterlilies and bullrushes, too, have almost disappeared.

According to where you happen to moor while cruising the Broads, the outlook can be empty and bleak or, alternately, serene and delightful: utter peace in a green world. Perhaps you might glimpse the last of the great black-sailed wherries carrying a happy band of passengers along the river ways where their kind once performed a flourishing trade.

Round the next bend may be a lonely mill, a patient fisherman or perhaps some leisure seekers lazily making their way along in a punt. Alternately, a busy centre where people are shopping or visiting the 'local' and perhaps watching the antics of would-be sailors – the creaking masts and flapping sails of their craft all mixed up with the sound of ducks and coots begging for scraps.

If you are very lucky you might catch sight of baby grebes cadging a ride on their father's back. Just occasionally there may be a mighty noise of huge wings as a father swan chases his young in an effort to make them leave home and start a life of their own. Half a dozen young swans all trying to take off together do make for a considerable commotion and a very dramatic exit.

I think of Broadland as a paradise of sights and sounds – and so it has seemed to me ever since I came into the world a century ago…

Contents

Sunrise at Thorpe Reach.

Philippa Miller.

Introduction

When the Norfolk artist and writer Philippa Miller died in 2002, she left my wife Philippa and I, as her executors, a number of hand-written and typed manuscripts, a substantial collection of paintings and sketches and several thousand photographs – all of which she had generated during her long life lived almost entirely in and around the Norfolk Broads. These words and pictures offered a very intimate but revealing account of Broadland from her birth in 1905 through to the immense changes to the nation and its people brought about by the Second World War.

Although 'Pippa' – as she was called by her friends – continued to record the highlights of her life in Norwich after she retired from teaching in the Sixties, it was her words and pictures of those transitional years from the end of Queen Victoria's reign to the middle of the twentieth century that struck both of us as being so invaluable in this new century, when so much of the past has been swept aside or lost from memory. She had lived through a time when the Norfolk Broads were still navigated by the old black-sailed trading wherries, when windmills and watermills still turned across the largely unspoiled landscape, and tourists had not yet arrived in the huge numbers that now flock to the area every year.

The Broads, as Philippa Miller knew them, were a place of isolation, tranquility and the beauties of nature in the wild, where sailors and yachtsmen could travel the rivers and waterways in almost solitary splendour and the motorcar had not yet blighted the towns and villages. As the daughter of a boat builder on Oulton Broad, she grew to love and cherish the area, helping in her own way to preserve some of the old sailing craft, drawing and photographing the last of the water and windmills, and generally recording the history of this part of East Anglia as it occurred and could be found commemorated in all manner of artefacts, from village signs to wartime pillboxes.

Little seems to have escaped her sharp mind and keen eye, her ever-present camera and deft pencil and brush. Undeniably, she enjoyed what was truly a 'Golden Age', and captured it painstakingly in words and pictures. What was surprising to Philippa and I was that she took all this trouble, expended so much effort and travelled hundreds of miles over many years, to satisfy herself. She exhibited very few of her paintings, mounted her photographs in dozens of neat little scrapbooks and wrote largely for her own information . A natural modesty prevented her from doing more.

To be suddenly confronted by this wealth of unique material after her death was both a delight and a challenge to us. She might have decided not to publish this work while she was alive, but we felt it deserved a much wider audience than the few friends and acquaintances with whom she occasionally shared her hard-won knowledge. It has, therefore, been a pleasure to compile this book and try, in doing so, to present the material as she would have liked.

No doubt if 'Pippa' knew of these plans, she would have smiled and dismissed the idea with the words, 'Now who would want to see my pictures and read what I have written?' My wife and I believe that when the reader has read and looked at the rich cache of words and pictures that follow – in truth only a fraction of the material she left – he will be in no doubt about the answer. The Norfolk Broads has had numerous chroniclers over the last hundred years, but few have lived and written about this era with greater insight, understanding and affection than Philippa Ruth Miller.

Peter Haining
November 2007

'At Play on Thorpe Reach' – a watercolour by Philippa Miller, c.1935.

Philippa Miller sailing the Broads, aged 6.

Chapter 1

Growing Up on the Broads

I was born on 10 January 1905, the first child of Fred and Susan Miller, who lived in a terraced house in Bridge Road, Oulton Broad, just a few hundred yards south of the Lowestoft to Norwich railway line. My father ran a boat yard on the Broad where he was kept busy building small yachts and launches for hire. In between breaks from caring for me, my mother used her artistic skills to carve nameplates for the boats – many of which were named after flowers. She also made curtains for the tiny windows of the craft and pennants to fly on their bows and mastheads.

As a wedding present, my father had given my mother – who was also known as Daisy – a slim and elegant rowing boat known as a skiff, and she delighted in taking friends around Oulton. Sometimes she ventured as far as Fisher Row, a beauty spot just beyond the confines of the Broad that was right beside an unusual feature for this part of the world – a hill.

There were times, too, when Fred and Susan went sailing together and explored further afield, either turning towards Beccles or continuing onwards to Somerleyton. The waters were good for sailing, with few trees to keep off the wind. There were endless delights to see: reed beds, an ancient windmill or two, with moorhens or ducks for company.

Opposite our house was a row of shops. Linder's, the sweet shop, Beckett's the draper and hardware emporium and Chipperfield's the butcher. Among a row of cottages nearby there was one that had been turned into a shop. Here old Mrs Hunton served her customers all sorts of groceries and vegetables. Opposite the door was a large barrel supported on its side on a trestle with a tap at one end from which hung a child's seaside bucket. From this Mrs Hunton dispensed thick black treacle to her customer's in jam jars, any drips falling into the bucket.

A few hundred yards away was Harrison's corn mill and beyond that a winding and rather rough passage which provided a short cut to Commodore Road and 'Miller's Yard' – as my father's yard was described on a large sign hanging on the water side of the buildings.

My father had fallen in love with boats and the Broads when he was a teenager and had bought his first craft, an open boat 16 feet long of clinker construction, when he was just 16. Inspired by a book, *The Land of the Broads*, written by the yachtsman and explorer, Christopher Davies, he rigged a mast and sail on his boat and set out to do his own exploring as far as the northern Broads and even the dangerous waters around Yarmouth.

Sometimes Fred would take along a couple of friends and they would stay out all night, sleeping under a makeshift awning. When the boys found this a bit cramped, my father built a small cuddy, but the height was so low they had to crawl in, as there was no headroom.

It seemed only natural to Frederick Miller that he

The Marguerite *– Susan Miller's little boat*

The London to Lowestoft Railway line at Lake Lothing.

Miller's Boat Yard, 1911.

should learn the skill of boat building, and he joined the firm of Robert Kemp at Oulton Broad. Kemp built various different craft, including several wherries, and later bought an ex-trader turned pleasure cruiser, the *British Queen*, built by Halls of Reedham in 1873.

My father was a hard-working young man who obviously learned his craft quickly. When not busy, he loved to ride a penny-farthing bike and took part in a number of races around the streets of Lowestoft. In one race, in June 1912, from the North Parade to the Hopton Hart and back, he finished second.

According to a newspaper account at the time,

'The Saltside' – a sketch by Philippa Miller.

Penny Farthing Race, June 1912. Frederick Miller is in the centre.

over 2,000 people lined the streets to watch the competitors riding along the eight-mile route. I was too young to watch, but my mother told me the riders were quite a sight as they competed against each other, battling through deep dust on their solid rubber tyres. Apparently, there was considerable betting on the outcome with a man named Barker at six to four on and my father at three to one. Fred finished in a time of 35 minutes and 24 seconds, which was less than a minute behind the winner.

I have also been told that during the very hard winter of 1885, when my father was just 22, he skated from Oulton Broad to Beccles and back by moonlight. It must have been a very thrilling experience, with only the sound of the skates cutting into the ice as he sped along.

Around the turn of the century – and after several years working in partnership with Robert Kemp – Frederick Miller bought out the business and was soon making his own mark on the sailing industry. In 1901 he built and raced a motor launch in the first ever race for motor launches to be held in Britain.

The year in which I was born, he also built a vessel, the Napier Major, which soon afterwards made the longest recorded trip by a motor vessel from Oulton Broad to the Orkney Islands. That same year he installed the first commercial engine in a drifter belonging to the Lowestoft fishing fleet.

I have a newspaper cutting dated September 1908 with a photograph showing my father on the Broad with the very first hydroplane to be designed and run in British waters. The report says that the Brooke hydroplane *Surprise* was 13 feet long, 56lbs in weight and powered by a 12hp engine. It was capable of

BRITAIN'S FIRST HYDROPLANE ON THE WATER.

The Brooke hydroplane Surprise, the first to be designed and run in British waters. Thirteen feet long, and only 56lb. in weight without her 12-h.p. motor, she skims along the surface of the water at well over twenty knots an hour, and when going at full speed the hull is almost entirely clear of the water.

built by F. Miller   Sept 1908

Newspaper account of the Brooke hydroplane
Surprise, September 1908.

skimming along the surface at 20 knots and when travelling at full speed lifted almost entirely clear of the water.

As I grew up, I loved to go sailing with my father or else watch him and his men building and repairing boats in his huge black-tarred shed. It was also a great place for my younger brother, Martin, and I to play hide and seek – venturing across the tie-beams high above the huddle of boats below, quite oblivious to danger, as the young usually are!

I think Martin and I were often a trial to Frank Colby and Fred Jillings, who worked for my father in the yard for many years. But Frank and Fred were typical good-hearted men, who would just gently chide us in their thick Suffolk accents as we scurried about above their heads.

Frederick Miller's Tri-Car with wife, Susan, on board.

My father had one contrivance in his yard that always intrigued me. It was the equivalent of a large, long, square wooden tube, supported on legs about five feet high. Near one end was a boiler, which produced steam when a fire below it was lit, and directed this into the tube. Planks of wood were then thrust into the tube and steamed until they were pliable enough to be curved round the ribs of a partly built hull. They were then riveted into place and produced the slightly downward and graceful curve of the upper timbers of a boat. But as I recall, the plans actually had to be shaped beforehand in a gentle upward curve – the opposite direction!

Soon the business of Frederick Miller was expanding and his fleet of yachts grew in size. He began building motor launches for hire and, as the need for more space increased, he purchased the derelict makings and sidings on the adjacent property. A large new sign, 'Miller's Yacht Station', was put up outside and this could be seen all over Oulton Broad.

Fred also acquired a couple of unusual vessels. One was the old Southwold to Walberswick ferry, which he used as a floating mooring at the yard, while the other was a Thames barge which he converted into a 'floating hotel' to cruise the Broads. He called her the *Pauline*, of which more later.

As well as being busy at the boat yard, my father had a chandler's shop opposite the end of Commodore Road beside Mudford lock, over which was a bridge that carried the main road from Oulton Broad to Beccles. Behind the shop was a rough, sandy track running by the estuary to Lowestoft, past shipyards, old posts green with weed, by pebbly shores all along what was known as the 'Salt Side'. Salt or not, swans in great numbers used to congregate there within sight of the lock and the main road.

Oulton village, separate from that of Oulton Broad, was mainly to the north of the Broad and was known as the Rock Estate. We became familiar with the area when going to St Michael's Church or to functions held in the Institute.

In order to reach the Institute, I had to walk from Miller's Yard along a cinder path, up steps and over a wooden bridge that spanned the rail tracks, and past Swonnell's Maltings. Occasionally, I visited the Maltings and was allowed to go inside and see the great mounds of roasted barley, fresh from the oven, all giving off warmth and a delicious smell.

There were other roads on the south side of the railway line, which curved past the richer homes lining the edge of the Broad. In the past, George Borrow of Lavengro fame had lived in the district, as had Lieutenant-Colonel Back, the chairman of Back's the wine merchants, who had a fine house on the hill called Mancroft Towers.

Miller's Chandler Stores, *a sketch by Philippa Miller.*

A Miller family tea-party, 1912.

'The British Queen' – a watercolour by Frederick Miller, c.1900.

'Wherry on Reedham' – a watercolour by Frederick Miller, c. 1914.

'Lowering the Mast at Ludham Bridge' – a watercolour by Susan Miller, c.1911.

The Fleet at Anchor on Oulton Broad.

Fred Jillings at work on a Miller yacht.

The Miller extended boatyard on old maltings land.

Launching the impressive Gondolier.

The Millers' 'Speedy Wing' motor cruiser.

'Floods' – a watercolour by Philippa Miller, painted near Burgh Church.

Inset: *'The Floods at Burton Lammas'*
– a sketch by Philippa Miller.

Rescue boats in the flooded streets of Norwich, August 1912.

The ancient windmill that overlooked Oulton Broad in 1871.

On Sundays my parents would walk to Oulton Church, a mile or so away through country lanes. St Michael's was an ancient and interesting building with a central tower and stood on a rise overlooking the marshes and the river. It was not long before Daisy began playing the organ there, for she was already an accomplished pianist.

Sometimes, at weekends, they would go out for a ride in Fred's tri-car, a kind of motorbike with a basket chair in the front. I remember that once, when my mother was suffering with her back, a remarkable thing happened. The tri-car went rather quickly over a hump-backed bridge and it seems that Daisy's vertebrae clicked back into place!

Father taught me to swim and sail almost as soon as I learned to walk. Before long I was sculling around in an old rowing boat – by 'sculling' I mean using one oar that is placed in a semicircular slot in the stem board. By weaving the oar from side to side I could maintain a fairly straight course at speed.

In 1911 we moved into 'The Old Mill House' on Commodore Road to be nearer to my father's business. The house was situated on land above the boat sheds near the northeast corner of Oulton Broad. An old engraving my father had showed that in the past there had been a tall windmill on slightly rising ground just behind the house, but the only indication of it at this time was an old millstone that acted as our back doorstep.

The house was square and squat, whitewashed with a slate roof, and had two small lawns at the front. At the back were a paved yard and a small, brick-built privy, complete with two-hole seat and buckets beneath. In those days, of course, cut-up sheets of newspaper hung from a nail for use after any visit.

I was sent to school in Lowestoft to a little private school in the High Street. It overlooked wasteland far below the cliffs, called the Denes, where fish-ermen hung their nets to dry over a forest of poles. Beyond this we could see the sea – which, incidentally, used to be called the 'German Ocean'.

At this school, various little boys and girls like myself received the rudiments of education. I remember very little about my time there, except that one afternoon a week we had to write home and when I couldn't think of anything to say, I would write a fairy story or draw a little picture. I do remember once being frowned on by the head-mistress when she saw me walking home without wearing my gloves. I was only six!

In 1912, after a miserable summer, there were unusual gales and disastrous floods due to excessive rain on one single day. On the morning of Monday, 12 August, the skies over Oulton Broad were grey and sodden and a pitiless rain fell and strong winds blew in from the sea. Then, at 11a.m. there was dead calm. At 12.30 hurricane winds got up which broke down trees and caused boats at anchor to break their cables, battering one another on the stone steps.

The locks provided some shelter, but the water was soon cluttered with wreckage – oars, boat hooks, life buoys, sails, torn mooring ropes and halyards all in shreds. Dozens of boats felt the fury of the elements that day: dinghies were waterlogged, motor-boats sunk and sailing boats either foundered or were left lying on the rocks. Thousands of fish were cast ashore and in the surrounding district, the carcases of cattle floated down the river. The number of roof tiles and telephone poles brought down was beyond calculation.

Many areas of the Broads were flooded as a result of the storm, and parts of Norwich were under several feet of water for days, transforming the roads into rivers. People had to be rescued from their swamped homes by boat, and many brave men risked their lives to get food to others trapped in their houses by the deluge. The first lull in the storm did not occur until 5p.m., when the people of the Broads began counting the cost.

The storm naturally caused great damage and difficulties to my father's business. A number of his growing fleet of craft for hire were damaged and it meant many hours of extra work for him and his reliable old assistants, Frank Colby and Fred Jillings.

Two years after the great deluge the First World War began. This meant the end of my schooling in Lowestoft, and my parents arranged that I should attend a school near my home run by a Miss Flack in the upper room of a villa just around the corner from Commodore Road.

The difficulties and restrictions due to the war soon began to take effect. My parents had to have soldiers billeted on them at 'The Old Mill House' and a shortage of food was noticeable to everyone – especially a growing girl like myself. Apart from being difficult to get, the margarine was quite horrible and there was something else called 'honey-sugar' that was equally unpleasant. But we were still luckier than some, in that our soldier guests were able to supplement our rations – especially at Christmas.

The bitter fighting in the trenches on the European battlefields and the terrible lists of killed and wounded did not directly affect us, as my father was too old to join the forces and my brother was too young. But a Mr Cook and his son, who were friends of my parents, joined the Army and one of them was killed in the fighting.

For a time, the only indication we had that a war was going on was the fleet of Belgian fishing boats that were moored on Oulton Broad. They would remain there in silent rows until the conflict came to an end.

In 1915 the war the war did come our doorstep by way of German warships shelling the east coast ports. One huge piece of shrapnel landed on our property· it was heavy and dangerously jagged. Also, a giant airship, a Zeppelin, meandered along the coast from Southwold to Yarmouth dropping bombs on Lowestoft and district, setting fire to Laten's timber yard and causing considerable damage to a number of houses, although no lives were lost.

When such raids occurred, we all had to hurry down to the cellar below the kitchen. I remember during one alarm that one of the boys in khaki who was billeted with us calmly went on putting on his shiny brown boots and his puttees by the light from the slit window at ground level. We were all under the table!

Probably the closest shave we had in Oulton Broad was during a bombardment by the German Navy in 1916, when a shell hurtled through a row of terrace houses in Kent Road. It shot through the first house, then a second and third, and on until it had flown straight through the middle of 13 houses! Amazingly, no one was injured – although several people had narrow escapes. The shell was eventually picked up unexploded under the bed of a little boy in the thirteenth house. The number was obviously lucky for him!

AIR RAIDERS ON EAST COAST

BOMBS ON LOWESTOFT & SOUTHWOLD

TIMBER YARD ABLAZE at LOWESTOFT

THE TOWN SHAKEN

STORIES OF MIRACULOUS ESCAPES

THREE HORSES KILLED.

FIRE BOMBS ON HENHAM HALL

FLIGHT ALONG NORTH NORFOLK COAST

Early this morning the East Coast was the scene of a Zeppelin raid. Shortly after one o'clock an airship was sighted off Lowestoft, and it passed over the town, dropping six bombs and setting fire to Messrs. Latten's timber-yard. The explosion of the bombs and the sounding of the fire alarm aroused many of the inhabitants, but there was no panic. Three horses in a stable on Denmark Road were killed, but happily there was no loss of life among the residents.

The houses in Denmark Road from the Suffolk corner to beyond Trafalgar Street had their windows smashed, and of his bedroom was wrenched from its hinges and blown bodily on to the bed. Fortunately the occupant escaped injury. The window and all the crockery in the room were smashed. The upstair rooms were slightly damaged. The occupants were naturally scared at the falling glass and the breaking of the doors, but they themselves escaped without a scratch. The houses to the right and left of No. 48, Denmark Road, were also damaged, and the occupiers were terribly frightened by the sound of the smashing glass, but, as far as can be ascertained, no one suffered serious injury. Some smaller houses to the rear of this spot, a Junction Passage were also damaged as the result of the explosion. The window of Mr. Thirtle's hairdressing establishment was blown to atoms, while the other four cottages in the row suffered damage.

Latten's timber yard was badly damaged as the result of the outbreak of fire, which

Contemporary report of the German raid on Lowestoft in 1915.

An unexploded bomb of the type dropped by the Zeppelin.

One of the Zeppelins that raided Lowestoft

Belgian fishing boats moored on Oulton Broad during the war.

Path of the German shell that ended under a boy's bed in Kent Road, Lowestoft.

It must have been near the end of the war when a deep explosion was felt and heard one morning. This, we discovered later, was a munitions factory in Silvertown in London. It had been such a huge explosion that it was felt by all of us, some 100 miles away. The works were demolished, with 70 people killed and 400 injured.

Once the war was over, my father set about expanding his business. He increased his fleet of yachts and began building motor launches for hire. Soon he had to expand the quay heads to provide extra room for his growing fleet and make more space for a wide runway to launch his bigger boats, such as the *Gondolier*, one of the largest motor cruisers on the Broads.

In the early twenties, Fred Miller acquired a roomy pavilion situated behind the riverbank just beyond Fisher Row, near the first bend in Oulton Dyke. Here he opened a 'Chinese Tea House' and began offering refreshments to holiday visitors. He also built quays where they could moor their yachts and launches.

The necessary provisions for the restaurant were brought up by launch at regular intervals, and local people were engaged to help in preparing and serving teas or lunches. At the back of the large hall there was a counter and small kitchen and above that a tiny room that could be used as sleeping quarters if necessary. Often, at weekends or in school holidays, I would help there and bring a friend – we thoroughly enjoyed the open air and unrestricted life.

Outside the tearooms there was a swing and a rough grassy area for children to play. Beyond our land were marshes full of flowers – ragged robins and marguerites, even orchids – not to mention wild grasses and plenty of butterflies.

There was also a lovely walk from here to Fisher Row or, in the opposite direction, to Oulton Church and the village. Many a family out for a day, or those who were touring the rivers, would stop by at the tea gardens. My mother, who by now possessed her own little sailing boat, would bring friends up to see how the business was getting on – and no doubt to enjoy a cup of tea, too.

Once a young parson hired a small houseboat and moored it alongside the Chinese Tea House. That night he appeared in his pyjamas on our doorstep in Oulton Broad. He said his boat was filling with water and gradually sinking. My brother went to the rescue and soon found that he had moored so tightly that as the tide went down, the boat had leaned further outward while gently slipping water.

'Why didn't you use the pail to bale out and loosen the mooring ropes?' Martin asked him.

'I couldn't, could I?' the parson replied. 'My pail had drinking water in it and it took too long with the water bottle!'

On another occasion, a yacht ran full tilt into the soft reed beds and the occupants were frantically trying to push it off with their quant, which they were holding in quite the best position to push them further in!

My father was always happy to help and instruct would-be and newly fledged yachtsmen. I, too, enjoyed sailing and imparting what knowledge I had to friends, and would then photograph them handling the boats as to the manner born.

Around this time, my father took me to visit 'Scientific' Fuller, an old man who lived all alone in a rackety old houseboat almost buried in the weeds at Rockland Broad. He earned his living by fishing, trapping and wildfowling in his gun-punt, and was an encyclopaedia on any natural inhabitants of the area.

Among the stories told about 'Scientific' was that once, when the Broads were frozen for several weeks, he was challenged to shoot a black-headed gull while skating at full speed. Holding his gun in both hands, the old man waited until the gull wheeled above him, then skated after it. He brought his gun to his shoulder and fired, the gull dropping almost at his feet.

The Old Mill House, Oulton Broad.

Whenever I skated on ice I always thought of that story and marvelled at how skilled he must have been to be able to do the two things at once.

Each September, after father's letting business had practically finished for the season, we would go for a holiday on the *British Queen*. She was a converted Norfolk wherry, one of those huge, black-sailed traders used throughout the eighteenth and nine-

teenth centuries to transport goods between inland towns and coastal ports, mainly carrying grain or coal and timber.

The wherries were unique craft and were usually managed by one man and a boy, or a man and his wife, and were designed to sail 'close to the wind', which was very useful on the winding rivers of Broadland. The interior of our wherry – originally a large, open hold – had been converted into a lounge with two or three cabins, a toilet and kitchen facilities. It had an entrance hatch on one side and was comfortable and pleasant to sail in. The *British Queen* even had a piano on board.

The large sail was raised and lowered by one rope on a windlass. When unshipped, the counter-balanced mast could be lowered quite speedily – even by me – to enable the wherry to maintain way under the low-arched bridges to be found on some of the Broads. Occasionally I helped with the steering and even managed the giant quant pole when it was necessary to keep moving if the wind dropped. It took quite a bit of skill to plunge it in at the correct angle, allowing for the speed and drift of the wherry.

We would often moor within reach of little village shops to replenish our provisions. I remember one occasion when, gliding up the narrow reaches of the River Chet, we stopped by the bank where a cow was being milked and bought some warm, fresh milk for breakfast.

Some early mornings, before the mist had lifted,

Military guests of the Miller family at The Old Mill House.

Top: *Pretty Fisher Row.* Above: *Views of Miller's tea garden on Oulton Broad.*

Above: *Views of Miller's tea garden on Oulton Broad.*

Frederick Miller greeting visitors to his 'Chinese Tea House' on the Broads.

Susan Miller and the choir of St Mark's Church, Oulton Broad.

Miller family and friends on the British Queen, 1915.

A typical cruising party on the British Queen.

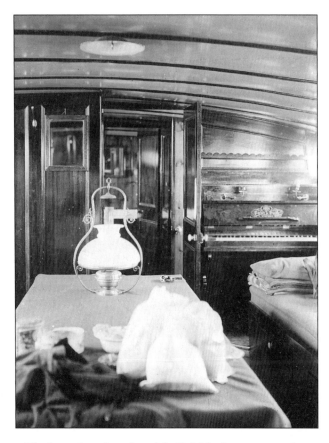

Top and above: *Races underway at Oulton Broad Regatta, 1931.*

The luxurious interior of the British Queen, *complete with piano!*

father and I, not having bathing costumes, didn't bother with them and enjoyed a refreshing dip. There were mushrooms and blackberries for the finding on those trips, and sometimes a convenient pub by the water's edge. At any of these it was possible to get a welcome lunch, with superb raspberry pies and lashing of cream.

I have very fond memories of those carefree days on the *British Queen*. Sadly, like many of her kind when the railways and road haulage took over their trade, the old wherry had to be laid to rest. In 1925 her black sail was hoisted for the last time and she was sailed to Lake Lothing and scuttled. She was just 52 years old.

The twenties and thirties saw the growing popularity of the Broads – leisurely, lonely and delightful. Soon there were all kinds of annual events being held at Oulton Broad and Beccles, including regattas, races and carnivals. For one of these my brother and I dressed up in Chinese costumes and erected a huge but flimsy Chinese lantern on an old rowing boat. I think we won a prize and certainly we amused a lot of people.

Sailing races were starting to become popular and were always very graceful to watch. At the same time there was all the bustle and excitement of the

occasion to be enjoyed. A gentleman's estate on the south side of Oulton Broad was turned into a public pleasure ground and named, in his memory, the Nicholas Everitt Park. It quickly became an excellent place for people to enjoy fêtes, watch the races or take refreshment.

As a family, we always made a special effort to go each year to the Beccles Regatta. We usually took one of our larger launches and moored beside the riverbank close to all the festivities. This enabled us to watch in comfort from – so to speak – our own grandstand. There were sailing races and water sports of several kinds, including a 'football match' played by swimmers with goalposts about 18 inches above the water level.

The great attraction on shore was a fairground set up on the quay. There were any number of stalls, coconut shies, fortune tellers and, of course, the 'horses' on the roundabouts – most of which, I seem to recall, were ostriches. We never missed a ride on any of them, enjoying the riot of noise and colour and happy laughter. The Beccles Regatta was always a great family day out.

When he had time, my father liked to relax by painting the Broads and its scenery. He was completely self-taught, but showed considerable talent in his paintings of the rivers and boats. I shared his enthusiasm, and sometimes I would borrow one of his yachts and go off with friends to sail and sketch. We travelled quite long distances, but never across the wide stretches of Breydon Water to reach the northern rivers, for it would have taken more time and ability to negotiate the fast-flowing

Speedboat Miss Phyre *with her creator, Martin Miller, at the wheel.*

Four inch model of a 'Fleetwing Class' motor cruiser, made by Martin Miller.

Boats jostling for position at Beccles Regatta. 1932.

tide speeding through Yarmouth on its way to the sea than we at that time possessed.

In 1927 Martin joined in the Miller business. He soon proved himself capable of handling any boat and coping with their engines, as well as designing new cruisers. A couple of years later he built himself his own speedboat, that he named *Miss Phyre*. He loved to speed around the wide expanses of the Broads, usually with his faithful companion, Rajah, the largest and gentlest Alsatian you could wish to find.

Martin designed some of our larger motor cruisers, too. He made an accurate, foot-long model of one of these for our agents in London, Messrs

The Chinese lantern boat built by Philippa and Martin Miller.

Blake & Co., to use as a showpiece and working model to attract tourists to the Broads. My own more modest contribution to the business was to design

Designs by budding artist Philippa Miller for the family firm.

displays for the front of our premises, as well as helping to produce little brochures advertising our yachting holidays.

Father would have liked me to go into the family business, too, but I am afraid that – backed by my mother, who knew that I was not very keen on working at a job where the hours were completely unpredictable and the busiest times would be when everyone else was having holidays or enjoying long summer evenings – I decided on trying for a career using my ability in art, which I seemed to have inherited from both my parents.

In any event, during the years that followed, father had the help of several different partners in his business. The Robinsons, Leo and Jack, branched out successfully on their own. Then there was one of my cousins, Maril Miller; Gordon Money, my mother's cousin, and Stanley Smith, who joined us for what would be the last few unhappy years.

The onset of the Second World War sounded the

end for F. Miller & Co. It put a stop to yachting holidays, for no visitors were allowed within two miles of the coast. The demand for new yachts and motor craft also slumped and no one sailed up to the Chinese Tea House any more.

My brother, Martin, became unwell and, with my father approaching his eighties, he decided to close down the business and retire. In 1940, Martin so wanted to join in the evacuation of Dunkirk – especially as our motor launches were readily available – but he was too ill and died a few months later in January 1941. In 1943 Frederick began to fail in health and in October 1943 was admitted to hospital in Norwich. He died later that month.

I like to think that the memory of Frederick Miller, the ship yard he ran and the boats he built, lived on because of the part he played in that first half of the twentieth century, helping to turn the Norfolk Broads into a mecca for sailors and yachtsmen that is now known all over the world.

Chapter 2
Pictures of Life in Lowestoft

During the winter months it was the custom of the Miller family to make regular trips to Lowestoft, the nearby fishing centre and tourist resort. There we would go to the pier or walk along the beach, enjoying the air and the sights. Alternatively, we would head for the quays that were always a hive of activity whenever the fishermen brought in the harvest of their hours of trawling the dark ocean waters. The row upon row of fishing boats tied up in the harbour, still wet from the lashing of the North Sea waves, were jammed so close together it was said you could walk from one side of Lowestoft to the other by just clambering over them.

Sometimes if we were there in the early morning, the dozens of drifters tied up at the quayside would be in the process of disgorging their catches of herrings. Thousands of gleaming, silvery fish could be seen being hoisted up from the holds in huge baskets. Then they would be landed, weighed and dispatched to where the ranks of 'fisher girls', with their huge wooden caskets, were waiting for the creatures they referred to as 'silver darlings'.

They were Scots lassies from places as far distant as Aberdeen, Banff and Stornaway, who came down for the work each winter and were a marvel to behold. They could gut a herring at great speed, packing it into the caskets filled with salt in a blur of

'Sunday in Lowestoft Harbour' – a pencil sketch by Philippa Miller, c.1925.

Packed South Beach, Lowestoft, on a Bank Holiday.

Scenes of holidaymakers on Lowestoft beach in the early thirties.

hand action. Speed was obviously of the essence, as the fish had to be hurried off to market in London. The whole process would be carried out amidst a cacophony of noise, with the heavy-booted fishermen shouting orders, the gutting girls emitting a constant stream of cackling and gulls screaming everywhere as they swooped to pick up any fish that went astray.

Despite our association with the water and sailing, the Miller family never tired of looking at the sea-going vessels and the sturdy fishermen who sailed them out to earn their living in all kinds of weather. We all liked herring, too, and I remember that it was possible to buy a 'string' of 20 fish for a 'tanner' – six old pence

If we happened to visit on a Sunday, the scene would be quite different – for the girls were deeply religious and would never work on the Sabbath. The fishermen, too, took the opportunity to fix their nets, service their boats or just sit on the quay smoking

and swapping experiences.

Like many other ports, Lowestoft had 'adopted' its own warship, HMS *Godetia*, and whenever an 'Open Day' was held so that visitors could go on board and see what life was like, there were always huge queues of curious men, women and children. Later, I remember that the town had the honour of being associated with HMS *Renown*, which took Winston Churchill to one of his famous summit meetings

The bustle and activity in Lowestoft harbour never failed to fascinate me, and I often took my sketchbook along to catch the moment. There were so many faces full of character that it was difficult to decide which one to draw. The smell of the fish permeated the whole area, and I frequently still had it in my nostrils, even on my clothes and my sketchpad, when I got home!

Such visits to Lowestoft in the winter were in marked contrast to summer outings whenever my

Reverend Peele and his East End Kids meeting the sea.

A windy day on North Beach, Lowestoft.

A quiet corner of Whapload Road, Lowestoft.

The first Lowestoft tram.

father was able to get away from the demands of the boat yard. Then we would make the most of a hot summer day and revel in the various entertainments. We enjoyed strolling along Marine Parade and Wellington Esplanade, though if we felt really energetic we might walk along the spectacular Denes.

A visit to the pier was always a must, and listening to the resident dance band playing popular music. When I grew older I was allowed to go to dances in Lowestoft with a friend, Nora. It was all waltzes and polkas in those days. I remember one evening in particular when Nora and I danced and danced until we had to run to catch the last bus home to Oulton Broad – happy but absolutely exhausted.

The family liked going to the theatre and cinema in the town to see the latest films. Also, we frequently shopped at Tuttle's, the drapers opposite the station, or Spashett's, a little further up the street. Later we became familiar with the first Woolworth's – though there were 'Penny Bazaars' long before that.

My father, of course, enjoyed the annual yachting events held off Yarmouth. He would go to the yacht club to meet his friends for a drink. Martin and I more often than not watched the races from the pier – which gave us a chance to slip away and enjoy the amusements when nothing was happening at sea.

Three elderly maiden aunts, cousins of my mother, lived in North Lowestoft, and we occasionally visited them. They were obviously straight out of *Cranford* and delightedly took us into their front room – their 'drawing room' – and offered us refreshment. They had always been as poor as the proverbial church mice and when, in later life, they were left money in a legacy, it seemed that the habits of a lifetime could not be altered.

The High Light over Lowestoft.

From top: *Holidaymakers and a rising tide under Claremont Pier.*

'High Light, Lowestoft' – a watercolour by Philippa Miller, c.1925.

They poured tea daintily into beautiful little china cups and got out the cake kept especially for such occasions. I remember one visit in particular. They offered my mother and I pieces of the cake with loud protestations that they could not possibly have any themselves. 'Oh, no, that would be greedy,' they said together, 'the cake is for dear Daisy and Pippa.' Their eyesight was obviously less than perfect, for not one of them noticed that the cake had already begun to turn green.

Other memories from that time remain a rather different shade of green in my mind. The running of the first tram in Lowestoft brought out hundreds of people to line the route. It ran for about two miles in a northward direction from the station in the centre of Yarmouth to the terminus at Belle Vue Park.

There was quite a rush to get on board that first run, but most of the seats on the open upper top had been reserved for the town dignitaries. As no one got off at any of the tram stops, there were a few grumbles from ordinary townspeople, who had come along hoping to experience this new form of transport for themselves

The long sweep of golden beach at Lowestoft was a favourite with visitors, and many pleasure cruisers stopped at the pier to off-load day-trippers. These came in all shapes and sizes. A local clergyman, Reverend Peele, became quite famous for his charity

A peaceful spot in Kensington Gardens, Lowestoft.

HMS Godetia – *Lowestoft's own warship, 1931.*

Awaiting a rider.

A view of Lowestoft Harbour, 1931.

work and regularly made collections so that poor children from the East End of London could spend a day by the sea.

It must have been an astonishing day out for most of them – because many had never seen the sea before and had no idea that was where fish came from! I imagine that very few of them could swim, and as many came from homes with no running water it may have been difficult to encourage them to go in the sea or even paddle in the surf!

When I was 12, I joined the Lowestoft Girl Guides, which had just been formed. Before long I became a patrol leader and dutifully learned my knots and the various rules and conditions, as well as accumulating several badges for different skills to decorate my sleeve.

Shortly after the First World War I was chosen to be the standard-bearer. We went up to London to attend the Peace Rally at the Royal Albert Hall. It was a most spectacular occasion, when we all assembled in the central area and, on command, dipped our company banners as one at the end of the ceremony. There were some 16,000 guides there from all over Britain and the Commonwealth.

The company held a number of camps, including one at Bridlington and another closer to home at Belton, near Yarmouth. I remember sketching the white cliffs and blue sky of the Yorkshire coast and making a number of studies of our days under canvas in the pinewoods at Belton.

In 1921, having decided on my future, I started training at the Lowestoft School of Art with the thought of becoming a teacher. Actually, I had been to classes there throughout my teens and taken the National Society of Art Masters examination each year. I even attended life classes, drawing nudes – much to the disapproval of one of the governors, I learned later.

The school, run by Miss Musson, was on the first floor of the Technical Institute, where many subjects were arranged for mariners and fishermen, then a fairly recent innovation. There were several rooms devoted to specialised subjects like textiles, antiques, still life and so on. I began working for the Oxford Delegacy of Local Examinations and had numerous subjects to tackle, including drawing and painting from life, perspective, lettering, portraiture, anatomy, embroidery and other crafts, as well as the History of Art and Architecture.

All this meant attending every weekday, including Saturday mornings and most evenings, guided by Miss Sergeant, Miss Varley and Miss Musson. Part of the time I returned as a pupil teacher to the Lowestoft Grammar School and occasionally found myself helping the Fifth Form Boys.

Above and right: *Outward bound – the herring fleet sets out.*

Homeward bound – trawlers laden with fish.

Home with the catch.

Landing the catch.

Arriving at Fish Wharf.

Gutting the herrings.

A pair of typical Scottish fisher lassies.

'A Scottish Fisher Lassie' by Philippa Miller, c.1931.

Roll out the barrel!

In the Clapham Road school there were various reproductions of classical sculptures, such as the Discobolus, Venus and a section of Greek frieze with acanthus leaves, and there was a skeleton. The boys introduced me to 'him' on my first visit to the life class already there. They expected me to shake hands – which I did!

I rather enjoyed the theories of perspective, and on one occasion I produced a simple design of a houseboat complete with reflections, accurately and mathematically sticking to all the rules. I also recall that when it came to tidying up at the end of each day, putting away all the boards and easels and such like, one of my jobs was to replace the fig leaves on the Greek statues!

Among the full-time students was a mature boy named Reginald Marlowe who sailed through his examinations and became a successful teacher of art. Another boy received a lot of good-natured teasing, as he seemed too innocent for words and very gullible. One of my original school friends, Ruby Neeves, worked with us and occasionally posed as a model for our studies.

During this time a number of us produced all sorts of handicrafts for sale to supplement our funds. We ran a little shop in a hut on Pakefield Cliff during the summer months, where it was easy for holiday visitors to find us. We were very busy, but still found time to enjoy the fun of the seaside or go to Oulton Broad, where we spent our time in and out of the water – not to mention on it in a yacht or launch borrowed from my father!

Salting the fish.

Resting on the Sabbath.

While I was training, some of the students became close friends, in particular Peggy Haas, who was a very clever artist, and Olive Craske, who achieved the distinction of having pictures hung in the Royal Academy. Sadly, both of them died tragically – Peggy developed an abscess on the brain, while Olive married a farmer and lived near Beccles for a time before suddenly committing suicide for no known reason.

At this time I made friends with two elementary school teachers who lived on my homeward route to the family home on Oulton Broad. We spent time taking holiday trips together – especially on my father's latest brainchild, a 'floating hotel' to cruise the waterways, called the *Pauline*.

We also discovered that it was very pleasant in the summer holidays to enjoy the sunshine and the view from the flat roof of the little conservatory attached to

'The Herring Boat Skipper' – a portrait by Philippa Miller.

the Old Mill House. From here we could see the Broad and all the activities going on there. To reach the roof, we had to climb up a ladder, and one summer a very sad thing happened – we lost a kitten. We could hear the little creature's plaintive mews and though we hunted desperately for it, it was never found. Many years later the mystery was solved when we discovered the kitten's little skeleton

hanging where it had been trapped between an old boat and the shed wall.

During my last year at Lowestoft Art School, I carried out a few commissions, such as letter headings for my father's firm, various small drawings for public use and a new design for the cover of the Lowestoft Guide, which was published to provide information for tourists. I had the idea of combining

Above: *Lowestoft Girl Guides.*

Guide camp at Belton.

Right: *Cover for the Lowestoft Guide by
Philippa Miller, 1929.*

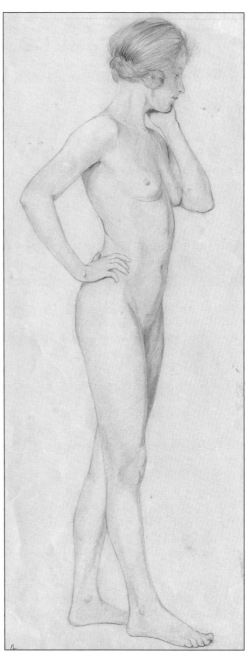

Above and right: *Two life studies by Philippa Miller that caused controversy at the Lowestoft School of Art.*

'Figure on the Stairs' – *a black and white sketch made by Philippa Miller at the Lowestoft School of Art.*

'Art Class' – *a sketch by Philippa Miller of fellow students at the Lowestoft School of Art, 1927.*

The Warren House and North Denes, Lowestoft.

'The Denes' – a watercolour by Philippa Miller.

a picture of the seaside with one of Oulton Broad and the wherries, yachts and cruisers that were now being seen there in increasing numbers. I thought it would show the range of attractions that holiday-makers could enjoy.

I provided a rough sketch of my idea and waited to see what happened. Imagine my joy when I received a letter to say that the Tourist Committee liked my idea and asked me to produce finished artwork. When the booklet was published in 1929, I was very proud to read in the local paper, the *Eastern Daily Press*, that 40,000 copies had been printed and the 'beautiful and arresting front cover' was from a painting by Miss P. Miller of Oulton Broad.

Chapter 3
The Forces of Nature

Living on Oulton Broad and close to the sea provided me with a constant reminder of the power of nature. The East Anglian coast has been known for centuries as the most vulnerable coast in Britain. Bitterly cold weather from the North Pole and the low, soft cliffs and many stretches of beach that have no cliffs at all, leave the area open to the onslaughts of the sea and the raging power of the wind and rain, especially during the winter months.

Three events in particular stick in my mind that occurred when I was a regular traveller between Oulton Broad and Lowestoft, and then to Norwich after I had become an arts and crafts teacher. First there was the frozen winter of 1929, then the damaging period of coastal erosion a decade later, followed by another bout of heavy floods in 1953.

The year that I began teaching produced a very severe winter – which also happened to coincide with my parents moving from The Old Mill House into a more up-to-date detached house on the opposite side

of the Broad facing the main road to Beccles. Though the house was more convenient, we still had a copper in the tiny kitchen in which to boil our clothes on washday, and there was still only an outside lavatory. The house was called 'Kya' – a corruption of 'a little house' in the Kaffir language, according to my mother's sister, who lived in South Africa.

The family were actually in the process of moving when the snow began falling. Soon the roads were impassable and Oulton Broad was completely frozen over. Skating then became part of the daily routine. In fact, we actually took advantage of the great freeze by moving a number of our possessions over the ice from one side of the Broad to the other.

Father and Martin were busy at this time designing boats for the Scouts in Scotland that were to be propelled by oars and/or sails. But my brother still found time to skate on the frozen Broad, and we took photographs of us all playing and walking on the ice.

The ice was solid almost all the way to Lowestoft

Oulton village under snow.

'Frozen Oulton Broad' – a watercolour by Philippa Miller, 1929.

Tobogganing through the village.

– though we had to be careful later when it began to thaw in some places, leaving great glistening sheets. Only then did it become possible to free the yachts and motorboats that had been frozen at anchor for weeks.

Quite a number of boats, and even property, was damaged by that severe winter – but nothing like the damage that was caused in 1938, when whole houses crashed into the sea at Pakefield where my student friends and I had earlier sold gifts to tourists. The coast there had been gradually eroded by the pounding waves of the North Sea until the little gardens on the cliff top had been eaten away. Then it was the turn of the houses to suffer the same fate.

Sea defences were being hurriedly put in place that year, but they came too late to help the houses on Beach Street. Heavy winter seas in the previous years had battered the sea wall below and undermined the foundations. Each day the people living there feared that a big storm would send them tumbling into the waves and so they abandoned the properties.

The family visited Pakefield and I took a photograph of mother on the cliff face. A short while later the spot where she was standing was no more – it had crumbled onto the beach below – and then after another bad night, the house nearest the edge collapsed. A photograph in the paper showed all that was left of the deserted home – the staircase, which had once been used for the family to go upstairs to bed, now ran down over the cliff. It was another tragic reminder of the power of the elements.

On 31 January 1953 these forces were let loose again when Norfolk suffered some disastrous floods. High winds and a sea surge towards the Channel

'An elephantastic snow monster' made by the author!

wrought havoc from Canvey Island to Lincolnshire. Many lives, human and animal, were lost, thousands of homes and shops were flooded, drains and sewers were put out of action and a number of piers, promenades and moored vessels were badly damaged.

The surge caused an extensive breakthrough of water at the marrams at Sea Palling and Salthouse, cutting a number of houses in two and leaving gardens and open spaces an absolute morass. Miles of marshes normally used for grazing cattle were inundated and made unusable because of the residue of salt after the water drained away.

My memory of this time is more personal, though,

Broken ice on Oulton Broad.

Miller's Boat Yard frozen up.

One sheet of ice.

The Broads – a frozen vista in 1929.

Another picture of Miller's Boat Yard becalmed in snow.

Martin Miller on the ice.

'The Frozen Winter of '29' – a chalk drawing by Philippa Miller.

and I always think of my brush with the elements as 'The Day when Gillingham was Flooded'. It happened on the Friday night when I caught the bus from Norwich to Oulton Broad in order to spend the weekend with my parents. The bus to Lowestoft conveniently passed my home – normally.

It was a winter night and getting dark as the bus left the city. Quite unexpectedly, when we reached Gillingham dam, the usual approach to Beccles, we found a crowd of people. The bus stopped and a man, obviously someone in authority, got on and said: 'Sorry, folks, the dam is flooded. The bus won't be able to go any further.'

We passengers all looked at one another. What on earth were we going to do out here in the middle of the night? Then, just as the man was just about to get off the bus, he added: 'Oh, there is a chap in a rowing boat who will be back soon who will ferry you across to Beccles.'

Thankfully, I picked up my luggage, got off the bus and waited with several other hopefuls. Before too long the 'ferryman' appeared with his boat and

three of us all immediately climbed aboard – despite his protestations that he had already done his last trip for the night.

There was a keen wind, scudding clouds and a moon that occasionally appeared in the sky in all its brilliance. One passenger was terribly nervous and sat in the stern with me, where I tried to comfort him about the safety of boat travel based on my own experiences.

For a while all went well, though we sometimes bumped into what was usually the roadside kerb and had to sheer away. Once we got stuck on a slight rise in the road level, but the ferryman managed to pull free.

On each side of us were pollarded willows and an occasional field gate, all standing knee deep in the flood. Before we were halfway across, our oarsman, who we now realised was 'merry' to say the least, lost direction and we drifted between two willows and out onto the open marsh.

Thinking I might be able to help, I steered while he concentrated on the oars, and we did manage to

Coastal erosion at Pakefield.

From top: *The floods at Gillingham.*

A house crashes down into the sea.

Right: *A wherry stranded in the floods at Potter Heigham.*

'The Moonlit Boat Ride' – a sketch by Philippa Miller.

Flooded fields near Beccles.

Windmill surrounded by floods at Somerton.

regain the road. Or rather the water above the road! At last, by the fitful light of the moon, we arrived beside the cottages near the river bridge, which now stood up like an island. The flood was halfway up the cottage doors. Here we had to get out while our ferryman turned round to go back.

A number of men were standing on the bridge in their wellington boots, watching and commenting on our arrival. One hefty chap offered to carry my nervous friend to dry land some 50 yards beyond. Another looked at how tall I was and didn't offer.

Remember, it was winter and the water was bitterly cold, so I didn't fancy paddling. So I brightly suggested that he should lend me his boots and I'd send the back with someone. To my surprise, he agreed!

I pulled the boots on and, to much hilarity, set off – but arrived at firm ground quite safely. There I gave the wellingtons to another man who was lounging about, with instructions to return them to my benefactor. Whether he ever did or not, I shall never know because he didn't seem in much of a hurry to move.

After this I walked up the street until I found a telephone box and rang my mother, because I knew she would be worried about me. She got out our car and came to fetch me. Was I thankful to be home that night – but what a tale I had to tell.

'Holidaymaking on the Broads' – a watercolour by Philippa Miller, c.1936.

Ready for the off on the Pauline.

Chapter 4
Holidays on the *Pauline*

The *Pauline* was a Thames Barge bought in the early twenties by my father, Frederick Miller, and converted into a 'floating hotel' to tour the rivers and broads of Norfolk in grand style. From 1923 until 1939 she offered an unrivalled opportunity for one to three week trips around Broadland for people who had no knowledge of handling a boat themselves or wanted the luxury of being conducted through the beauty spots of the area without having to worry about accommodation or catering.

Originally named *Federation*, No.113707, the barge was built at the Medway Cooperative Yard at Rochester in 1901. The 38-ton vessel regularly navigated the Regents Canal during commissions for Teynham brick makers until 1917, when she was sold to Wynnfield Shipping. They apparently found the barge unsuitable for their requirements after two years' service.

My father became the new owner and, with thoughts of turning the barge into a holiday attraction, fitted a Fay & Bowen 30hp petrol engine and re-named her *Pauline*. The boat was an immediate attraction from the day she first laid anchor on Oulton Broad.

Several cabins were built in the hold, which had once carried cargo, each fitted with bunks and cupboards, toilet facilities and lighting. Fred also created a saloon with cushioned berths, chairs and tables where the resident crew of three, a skipper, boy and cook, served meals and drinks throughout the journey.

The brochure, with its plan of the *Pauline*, that my father prepared for potential clients encouraged them to either book individually or get together a party of people who could hire the boat for a week or more. Apart from the usual home comforts – including a wireless (there was no television then!) – there was

Skipper Frederick Miller at the helm of the Pauline.

Holidays on the Norfolk Broads. The helmswoman on one of the new motor-wherries, which will be extensively used by holiday-makers this year. (S. and G.)

Above: *The author featured in the* Christian Herald, *3 May 1923.*

Left: *Up the creek!*

'Back in Harbour' – a watercolour of the Pauline *by Philippa Miller.*

Meet the Captain and crew!

Personally Conducted Tours

OF THE

NORFOLK RIVERS AND BROADS

ON THE

MOTOR CRUISER "PAULINE"

AT INCLUSIVE TERMS

OWNERS: F. MILLER & CO., LTD.

Special Terms to any Client Booking Whole Accommodation.

Motor Cruiser "Pauline"

The popularity of the Broads is increasing every year, but there are still many people who are unable to undertake a holiday on the Broads owing to insufficient knowledge of handling a boat, being unable to arrange a party, or who wish to be relieved of the worries of catering, etc.

It is for these people in particular that the "PAULINE" has been put into commission.

The "PAULINE" is comfortably fitted out with saloon, single and double cabins to accommodate 12 persons, and a select crew comprising:—skipper, steward and stewardess.

Individual accommodation may be booked.

Inclusive terms each person.

	£	s.	d.
During August	5	0	0
Other Months	4	0	0

SEPARATE ILLUSTRATED BOOKLET CONTAINING FULL PARTICULARS SENT ON APPLICATION.

Advertisement for holidays on the Pauline.

"The Ideal Holiday"

The popularity of the Broads is increasing every year, but there are still many people who are unable to undertake this holiday, owing to having insufficient knowledge of handling craft, being unable to arrange a party, or who wish to be relieved from worries of catering, etc. It is for these people in particular that MESSRS. F. MILLER & CO., have put the "PAULINE" into commission, as individual accommodation can be booked on this boat.

The Motor Cruiser "Pauline" is the largest passenger boat on the Broads, and is comfortably fitted out to accommodate 12 passengers. On reference to the plan, it will be seen that there are 6 single berth cabins, 2 double berth cabins and one cabin with 3 single berths, fitted with wash basins complete with water supply and waste pipe, and berths are fitted with spring mattresses, pillows, white blankets, sheets and counterpane. The saloon seats the whole party at meals, which consist of breakfast, lunch, tea and dinner. (Evening dress is not worn.) Good wireless set provided.

The interior is fitted with electric light throughout, and is well ventilated, having an average of over 7-ft. head room in saloon and cabins, with large open windows in each.

The crew includes a stewardess and good homely catering is carried out.

The whole idea of this holiday is freedom, fun and fresh air, coupled with trips in small launch and dinghy, picnics, etc. The tours are arranged in easy stages, so as to allow ample opportunities for passengers to follow their individual tastes such as fishing, swimming, rowing, sketching or walking, but we do not bind ourselves to exact times of arrival at any town or village except at the week end. All official trips are included in the terms.

We have arranged a succession of 3 weeks' cruises, and it is possible for passengers to book for 1, 2 or 3 weeks, and board the "Pauline" at either Oulton Broad, Yarmouth, or Wroxham.

Anyone who appreciates a free and easy out-door life is assured of a most enjoyable holiday—"THE IDEAL HOLIDAY" as our previous patrons have described it.

The Management reserve the right to alter the routine, and will not hold themselves responsible for loss or inconvenience caused by any delay en route.

Arriving passengers can take up their cabins any time after 2 p.m. on Saturdays, or, as the "Pauline" does not leave until Sunday morning, they may board any time before then.

Passengers are asked to vacate their cabins before noon on day of departure. No mid-day meal is included for day of arrival or departure.

The following is a programme of the full 3 week's cruise, and is intended to give a general idea of the district covered. Stops will be made according to circumstances.

Itinerary 1.

Passengers board at Millers' Wharf, OULTON BROAD, cruise to Beccles, Geldston, Somerleyton, Reedham, Cantley, Bramerton Wood's End, Thorpe St. Andrew, Norwich, Brundall, Surlingham Broad, Buckenham Ferry, Rockland Broad, across Breydon Water to Yarmouth; altogether a distance of about 75 miles.

Correspondence can be called for at Post Offices as under:

Beccles—Monday.   Reedham—Tuesday.
Thorpe St. Andrew—Thursday.   Yarmouth—Saturday.

Itinerary 2.

Passengers board at YARMOUTH Yachting Quay, cruise to Stokesby, Acle, Thurne, Potter Heigham, whole day Picnic excursion in launch to Martham, Horsey Mere and Hickling Board, cruise to Ludham, St. Benet's Abbey, South Walsham Broad, Horning. Launch trip to Ranworth Broad, Salhouse Broad, Wroxham Broad, altogether a distance of 60 miles.

Correspondence can be called for at Post Offices as under:

Acle—Monday.   Ludham—Wednesday.
Horning—Thursday.   Wroxham—Sunday.

Itinerary 3.

Passengers board near Wroxham Bridge, whole day picnic excursions to Belaugh and Coltishall, cruise to Mouth of Ant, Barton Broad and Stalham, South Walsham Broad, Acle, Yarmouth Burgh Castle, St. Olaves for Fritton Lake, Somerleyton, Oulton Broad; altogether a distance of about 70 miles.

Correspondence can be called for at Post Offices as under:

Wroxham—Monday.   c/o Bridge Hotel, Acle,—Wednesday.
Yarmouth—Thursday.   Oulton Broad—Saturday.

The Country Postal Service being somewhat limited, and many village Post Offices a long distance from the river, we recommend that letters should be addressed "On board Motor Cruiser Pauline" and should arrive by first post at places on days mentioned in each Itinerary.

All enquiries relative to the cruise will be promptly attended to by the Owners, F. Miller & Co., Ltd., Oulton Broad, and passengers should advise the firm of approximate time of arrival at least 2 days in advance.

LUGGAGE—Please confine to suitcases, etc., **NOT LARGE TRUNKS.**

No dogs allowed.

See separate leaflet for dates and terms.

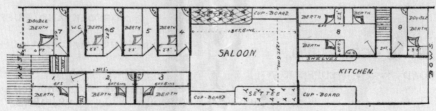

Itinerary for 'The Ideal Holiday'.

Above and left: *The* Pauline *motoring on the Broads.*

Below: *A picnic.*

no necessity, it was stated, for 'evening dress' to be worn for dinner.

There was plenty of space on the cabin top or deck to sunbathe – and as this was fairly high, the ever-changing scenery could be enjoyed with a minimum of effort. For those who wanted to be more active, fishing could be arranged or little trips on waterways in the *Pauline*'s dinghy.

I went on a few of the trips myself, and I can vouch that there was always something of interest to see on the busy waterways, from picturesque broads to a variety of other sailing craft and statuesque windmills. It was always possible to make stops at local inns and popular beauty spots, as well as visiting little villages from one end of the Broads to the other. Exploring the rivers of the Waveney, Yare, Bure and Ant was always full of unexpected delights.

Sometimes I was lucky enough to be able to take some of my friends on these trips and enjoy the care-free, outdoor life. Occasionally, too, I was even allowed to take the wheel by my father and felt like a real master mariner.

I remember being on board once when a young lad from Yorkshire was given the opportunity of steering the *Pauline*. His broad accent and invariably

The 'dining saloon' on the Pauline.

Boarding from the launch.

wind-swept appearance amused us. Once I asked him, 'Whatever has happened to your hair?' He replied, 'Ah, dawn't knaw – the win's all frizzled it oop into a poof!'

On another occasion we were supposed to be visiting Bungay, but had moored some distance away. At this, our Yorkshire friend said, 'Are we gooin' in the ding-ee to Boong-ee?' He didn't seem to

mind our outburst of laughter.

After my father stopped running holidays on the *Pauline* when the Second World War broke out, she was sold to a family who made her their home on Oulton Broad. Finally, though, like so many of her kind, the boat ended her days as staging on Barton Broad, a relic of a unique type of holidaymaking on the Norfolk Broads.

Chapter 5
Voyages of the *Nutcracker*

During the thirties, my resourceful brother, Martin, acquired an elderly yacht called the *Pelican*, which he converted into a delightful houseboat for me. There had to be plenty of headroom as I was nearly six feet tall, and he carefully made sure I was not in danger of hurting myself whenever I went on board. This little boat was to be my special passport to the Norfolk Broads, and over the years that followed there were not many miles of the rivers and waterways that I did not explore.

When Martin had finished renovating the boat it had a little deck aft and a tiny kitchen complete with oven, sink and pump. Inside the cabin were two tall cupboards – one serving as a larder and the other as a wardrobe – in between which was a six-foot bunk. Opposite this was a flat table and – most extravagantly – a little bronzed metal fireplace placed diagonally across one corner. Beyond were the bedroom, one double and one single bunk. To cap it all, my brother had installed in the bows a loo and a bath – the foot end of which was tucked under the fore deck.

Then came the great day when all was finished

The Pelican, *which was converted into the houseboat* Nutcracker.

'Interior of the Nutcracker*' by Philippa Miller, complete with fireplace!*

Conversion work progresses in Miller's Boat Yard.

The Nutcracker *is reborn!*

and I took my first journey on board my new 'home'. My father and Martin came, too, with the boat lashed to one of the Miller cruisers for the 28-mile journey from Oulton Broad to Thorpe, which was to become my base. Here, close to Norwich, suitable moorings had been found on the impressive sweep of the River Yare on the bank of a garden next door to Thorpe Old Hall, know throughout the area as the 'gem' of the

village's waterfront.

The owner of this garden was an undertaker. Imagine my surprise when I learned his name was… Mr Grief. But nothing could dampen my enthusiasm for my new *pied-à-terre*, and I decided there and then to call it the *Nutcracker*.

The boat was to prove a perfect retreat from my busy teaching life and also somewhere to entertain

Preparing the Nutcracker *at the moorings by Thorpe Hall.*

friends in a pretty riverside setting, especially in the summer. My family and relatives also came up from Oulton Broad and sometimes stayed on board for a while. This invariably led to busy scenes by day and quiet times on sunlit evenings or misty dawns. Our other visitors were either graceful swans or busy little coots and ducks.

It was always great fun to arrange firework parties on Guy Fawkes' Night. One 5 November, we set off some 'Golden Fountains' on several wooden planks and pushed them out into the river to make sure the sparks would do no damage. All the glory of the fountains was, though, reflected in the water as the planks floated slowly by.

About three yards away from my mooring was a tall, sheltering hedge and a small wooden hut, and in between these and the boat a grassy slope on which we could picnic or even hang out our washing. There was also a deep well with ample fresh water. It really was an ideal spot.

Thorpe Old Hall, with its lovely grounds next door, made a gracious setting. Edward Paston built the Elizabethan manor house in the late-sixteenth century on the site of the former summer palace belonging to the Bishop of Norwich. Later, when the Catholics were persecuted, its riverside position made it ideal for smuggling in priests by night, and there was said to be a priest's hole at the top of the stairs.

For years it was a favourite subject for the Norwich School of painters, and there were several owners during my time, including Commander Alfred Newhouse, Major Frank Astley Cubbitt and

Ready for adventure.

Beautiful Thorpe Reach.

his son, neither of whom did anything about adding electricity or bathrooms. It was later bought by the boat builders Jenners of Thorpe, who used part of the chapel building as an engine repair shop

I loved painting Thorpe Hall, with its ornate entrance and grand mullioned and transomed windows, which hinted at its rich history. But during the Second World War the place received a direct hit from an incendiary bomb that started its decline into decay. This was accelerated by vandalism, and in the 1960s it took two public enquiries to prevent it from being demolished.

The saviour of this romantic building was a Norwich businessman, Henry Burke, who bought the property for £1 and spent his fortune restoring the Hall to its former glory. In the process, mellow Tudor bricks were revealed under the modern rendering and these now change colour during the day to give the building a unique mellow beauty and charm. I hope future generations will enjoy looking at the Hall as much as I did when meandering by on the *Nutcracker*.

After a time I started a visitor's book on board my little houseboat. Some of the comments were amusing, while others were rather facetious. 'I have eaten far too much,' moaned one of my passengers, while another declared poetically, 'And still the wonder grew that one small boat so perfect was to view.'

Right: The entrance to Thorpe Hall.

'Thorpe Hall' - a watercolour by Philippa Miller, c.1935.

The Nutcracker *on the Broads.*

Afloat with friends!

Fishing for eels.

Fireworks at Thorpe!

A model of the Nutcracker *made by Philippa Miller.*

Easter and summer holiday times were ideal times to spend on the *Nutcracker*. I acquired a dinghy, and this enabled me and my friends to row down to the village stores in Thorpe St Andrews to get provisions or explore further afield. It was sheer heaven to drift lazily along, watching the yachting fraternity or the occasional wherry passing on the main rivers. Occasionally, when sailing from Oulton Broad to North Cove, we would find a quiet corner and perhaps exert ourselves to the extent of doing some fishing.

Once we moored beneath a gnarled willow on a lonely bank below Coldham Hall. Here we spent two weeks exploring the creeks and inlets in our dinghy, fetching the milk from the nearest village, fishing or sketching, watching the wild life in the early morning and late evening. Sometimes we amused ourselves observing the not always efficient holidaymakers and their navigational efforts.

I must add that the dinghy often needed attention, as it was rather ancient. Some of the planks needed reinforcing with a patch or two from time to time. It is wonderful what you can do with canvas and tar or a bit of caulking cotton when the need arises. The *Nutcracker*, too, needed painting and decorating on the outside to keep it waterproof and smart – 'ship shape and Bristol fashion', as sailors like to say.

There was huge tree at the mooring at Thorpe. It had an almost horizontal branch, but was a bit too high to reach. So some of my friends and I built a ladder and obtained a grand view of everyone coming and going. I remember being on the branch one morning and being startled to see my family coming up unexpectedly from Oulton Broad in one of the motor launches.

Another year we moored near the entrance to Rockland Dyke. Suddenly we found ourselves being admonished by the local landlord for stopping there. Actually, 'he' turned out to be a she, and when we put on our very best manners and apologised most profusely, the lady melted and invited us all to dinner that evening.

Rockland is one of the most unspoilt of all the Broads in my opinion. Shallow and wild, it was possible to watch swans gliding about their business and the fussy traits of the coots and moorhens. There were often reed warblers and water voles among the reeds, especially in early morning.

Sometimes we took our breakfast out in the dinghy, moored to a nearby stump or reed-fringed island, and cooked our bacon and eggs on the primus in the most perfect of sunlit mornings. When the primus was finally turned off and peace restored, it seemed there was nothing better than the delicious aroma of our food and the silent world all mirrored in the wide expanse of Broad.

When I look back on these outings with my friends, as we revelled in the unrestricted easygoing way of life on the water, I sometimes wonder why my memories are all of long days of sunshine. There must have been wet and windy days, surely!

Aboard the Nutcracker's *dinghy.*

69

'Wherry in a Green World' – a watercolour by Philippa Miller, 1930.

Two Norfolk Wherries at Bramerton on the River Yare, 1911.

Chapter 6
Rebirth of the *Albion*

During those long, lazy summer days half a century and more ago, I became very intrigued with the number of derelict wherries lying up in hidden waterways or sunk in reed-fringed dykes and weedy corners of the wilder parts of the Norfolk Broads. I was, of course, particularly interested in them because, from my childhood onwards, our family had their yearly holiday on board my father's pride and joy, the *British Queen*.

We had delighted in the unspoilt waterways of those early years, when the waters were crystal clear and wild flowers grew in profusion. Those unforgettable days of sail, peaceful and unspoiled, made me all the sadder to see these relics of the past seemingly abandoned and forgotten.

As I gazed at the wherries I was overcome by emotion and nostalgia. The cracks in their sun-baked planks, still visible above the water, had secreted an accumulation of mud and dust enough to allow mosses and lichens to grow on them. As if not to be outdone, the seeds of riverside plants – such as loosestrife and willow herb – had also found enough moisture to gain a foothold. In their abandonment, the rotting timbers of the old wherries had become charming wild gardens.

Many of these discarded hulks had been sunk deliberately to shore up the banks of the rivers. This had been done to lessen the damage being done by the wash of the motor cruisers as they swept by. But to me there was so much history and tradition in the wherries that they surely deserved better than these watery graves.

In July 1948 I wrote an essay, 'Norfolk Wherries', which a country magazine, *The Democrat*, published. It brought me some interesting letters from likeminded folk who were sorry to see the fate of these grand old boats, as well as some communications from a handful of old wherrymen and women. I was

A lone wherry on the Broads in 1934.

'The Last of the Wherrymen' – a watercolour by Philippa Miller.

A rare sight by 1939.

clearly not alone in my nostalgia for these black-sailed traders unique to Broadland in their type and construction.

The following year, a group of local Broadland people determined to keep afloat at least one genuine example of a wherry to preserve for posterity. Under the leadership of Roy Clarke, a local bookseller and historian (who later wrote the definitive book on *Black Sailed Traders* in 1961) a meeting was held on 23 February at the Stuart Hall, Norwich, to form the Norfolk Wherry Trust. In his speech about the plan to save a wherry and the need to raise funds for this purpose, Mr Clarke told his audience:

'We visualise a live, active vessel plying the waters on which the younger generation can set their feet and learn something of the sort of life, the sort of craft and the sort of men who raised our city and county to its current standing.'

He told the gathering, which included my teacher friend, Pamela Baker, and myself, that a potential craft had been identified: the *Plane*, built by William Brighton on the banks of Lake Lothing near Lowestoft in 1898. She had carried her first freight of 36 tons of coal from Lowestoft to Bungay, and continued to trade on the Norwich river until the Second World War. During the conflict she had been stripped of her gear and used as a lighter at the Colman's Mustard Factory in Norwich. She was lying there still, Mr Clarke said.

Suitably enthused, we 'Forty-niners' – as the original group who attended the inaugural meeting later came to be known – started by acquiring the *Plane*, which would later be renamed the *Albion*. She was

then the last remaining wherry still working, albeit only as a lighter.

We also needed somewhere as an HQ and were able to use the ancient and partly derelict tavern 'The Briton's Arms' in Elm Hill, although it was under the threat of demolition in the near future. It was in a sad state of repair, but we all set to and renovated the interior so successfully that the powers-that-be decided to complete the job and repaired the outside of the building. Later it would become a popular restaurant for people in the city.

So the Wherry Trust was formed – and, before long, after much voluntary labour, the *Albion* was re-born.

The *Albion* was fitted out with a new sail and all the necessary gear so that she could carry cargo. Later she would be let for the day or week for individuals or parties to sail the waterways for pleasure. Local Broadsmen were willing skippers, and soon the *Albion* began to earn her keep.

The Wherry Trust is now a going concern, with dedicated and unpaid enthusiasts keeping the good ship sailing. Her graceful lines, huge black sail and gay colours from masthead to deck attracted the attention of everyone as she sailed silently by on the river. By the time the *Albion* celebrated her centenary in 1998 she was without doubt the most photographed boat on the Norfolk Broads

After all the work that was put into restoring the *Albion*, it seemed only fitting that I ought to sail on the unique craft myself. So in 1968 I hired the wherry

A derelict wherry, the Spray, *once sailed by William Royall, near Postwick in 1936.*

for a day's cruising on the Broadland rivers through what was then being described as 'one of Europe's most important wetlands'. I invited 11 local friends and we set sail from the quay at Barton Turf, after the skipper and two 'cabin boys' had hoisted the huge black sail.

Soon we were moving downstream to Barton Broad, a vast sheet of water with old black marker posts and a reedy island. Beyond the broad and into the river we glided gently by flowery banks and beneath overhanging willows. Alongside us water birds scuttled into the reed beds or, like the ducks and swans, came eagerly towards us to snap up any titbits thrown to them.

An old trader almost lost from sight at Surlingham Broad.

Left to decay on Brundall Dyke.

Philippa Miller hunting for sunken wherries in the Broads.

The mysterious wherry No. 44, alone and abandoned.

A pair of rotting wherries at Hobrough Dyke.

'Nature's Garden' – Surlingham.

Under steam power: a wherry and lighter.

Top and above: A wherry in tow near Norwich with a lead weight on the end of the mast to provide balance.

The art of quanting.

Above and opposite: A unique series of photographs taken by Philippa Miller at Oulton Broad in 1936, when bad weather prevented a wherry from sailing.

An early pleasure wherry, 1913.

A trader arriving at Yarmouth in 1926.

As we sailed along enjoying the ever-changing scenery, bathed in sunshine, we became aware that ardent photographers on every other boat were doing their best to capture the *Albion* on film. I think we were even more of an attraction than the herons that can be seen – if you are lucky – flying overhead or standing motionless waiting for fish.

Broadland is a delightful playground – an area of little rivers leading to the larger Bure or the Yare and eventually to Great Yarmouth and the sea.

At intervals there are gaps or short dykes through which one can sail and discover open water – the broads proper – which were made long ago when large areas of peat were dug out for fuel. Today, they are fringed with reeds and willows and often enhanced with loosestrife, yellow iris or water lilies.

As the *Albion* sailed along, the lines of reeds with feathery tops rustling in the breeze were sometimes so tall that the landscape beyond was hidden. From our cabin top, though, it was possible to see the

The 'Save The Wherry' campaign that generated public awareness of the magnificent old traders.

A happy party of Philippa Miller's friends out for a day on the Albion.

A NORFOLK
TRADING
WHERRY

occasional windmill used to move water from over-full dykes in the grazing marshes out into the river. In the distance, sails of invisible yachts appeared to move across those same marches.

On that perfect day there was always something interesting to watch and nothing to disturb our serene progress in the hands of the capable skipper. Not even when we all had to manhandle our way under Ludham Bridge after lowering the sail and mast and then hoisting them all up again in order to proceed to our destination. I'm sure we had lunch and other refreshments during the journey – but it was so full of interest that I just don't remember anything so mundane!

Left: *'Norfolk Trading Wherry' – a pen and ink sketch by Philippa Miller.*

Chapter 7
In Search of Mills

Because my name is Miller it might be assumed that my interest in windmills and watermills followed naturally from this fact. In truth, that was not the reason at all. My mother, Susan, had been intrigued by them when she was growing up in Norfolk, and one of her earliest sketches, when she was just 15 years old, was of a post mill. I remember her showing me the fine ink sketch when I was in my teens, and I promptly took it as my inspiration to paint a watercolour of one of the mills we passed on the Broads during a trip on one of my father's boats.

The sketch was to prove the beginning of a lifetime of fascination with the stately giants that could then still be seen across the Norfolk landscape. In later years, during the thirties, while travelling about the Broads with my faithful camera, I snapped mills wherever I found them. I remember being particu-

larly impressed by the stubby post mills at Earl Soham, Wisset, Wrentham and Tacolneston, and the looming windmills at Thurne, Hunsett, Horning, Burgh St Peter, Ludham, Waxham Dyke and Potter Heigham. I am pleased to say that those photographs have survived the ravages of time very well – in some cases better than the windmills themselves.

It used to be said in Norfolk that only a fool would build a windmill if he could build a watermill. The argument was that by using water you had constant power and the opportunity to build a large and firm structure. Wind power, on the other hand, was erratic, and construction posed difficult engineering problems.

The sails, which were originally frameworks covered with cloths of coarse material, had to be capable of being moved so that they always faced the wind. In early mills, known as post mills – like the

The famous painting 'Mousehold Mill', by John Crome.

83

'Old Mill on Buckenham Marshes' – an evocative watercolour by Philippa Miller.

An old Norfolk post mill drawn by Susan Miller when aged 15.

Old water-pump on the River Ant, 1930.

St Olaves windmill, 1930.

one my mother drew – the solution was to move the whole structure by bodily swinging it in the wind using a long beam projecting from the back. Those early windmills may have been no higher than a man, but there was an incentive to build high. The higher the mill, the greater the span of the sails and the greater the power developed.

It then became apparent that there was no need for the whole mill to move round when the wind changed – all that was necessary was for the 'cap' carrying the sails to rotate. So this was put on top of a fixed tower and had a small 'fantail' set at right-angles to the main sails to ensure they were always facing the wind. A man named Edmund Lee invented this great improvement in 1745.

This development leads to the two major types of

'Broads Windmill' - painted by Philippa Miller in her teens.

windmill – the 'tower' and 'smock' mills. They are identical, except that the former are built of brick or stone and the latter, which are so called because of their resemblance to a farm labourer's smock, are made of wood. The sails also have a 'pitch' like that of an aircraft propeller, and the axis of the sails is sloped backwards. Later still, the shutters on the sails were made adjustable to catch more or less of the wind – another brilliant invention in 1772 by Andrew Meikle, the man who invented the threshing machine.

The climax of all this development was the building of large numbers of windmills in the nineteenth century. Some were designed specifically for corn grinding and others for drainage – and in their heyday they brought prosperity to many towns and villages in England. For a time there were over 10,000 working mills in the country – with Norfolk having among the most in any county

The county could also boast the highest windmill not only in England, but also Europe: the 12-storey Southtown tower mill built at Great Yarmouth in 1812. Measuring 122 feet to the tip of its cap and with a diameter of 40 feet at the base, the mill was capable of grinding a ton of wheat or 13 hundredweight of oats in an hour. When this giant was severely damaged in a storm in 1905 and sold off for demolition, the number of bricks that were salvaged was enough to build a row of houses known locally as Mill Cottages!

Mills of East Anglia: Thurne Mill.

Earl Soham post mill.

Hunsett windmill.

My father once told me a story that there were so many mills on a seven-mile stretch of the river between Norwich and Great Yarmouth that a group of men on a pleasure cruiser challenged each other to drink a pint of beer in the boat's bar every time they saw a windmill. Before the journey was halfway through, he said, the whole lot were lying drunk on the deck! He never revealed whether the party were on one of his cruisers!

There are lots of other stories about the windmills of the Broads. It was said that some mills were used by smugglers, who would position the sails in such a way as to warn their accomplices that the customs men were abroad. Several of the older mills were claimed to be haunted by the ghost of the miller. During the Second World War, a number of the mills were used as Home Guard lookout posts, and it was well-known that American airmen used them as landmarks when returning home from bombing missions over Germany: particularly those at Cley, Billingford, Thurne and – appropriately - Denver Mill.

Over the years, the windmills have been a favourite subject with artists – the great John Crome, for example, painted the post mill on Mousehold

Heath close to where I live – and thousands of visitors love to snap the remaining examples. The 'White Mill' at Thurne is widely believed to be the most photographed windmill in England, and I have never been able to resist taking yet another picture of this magnificent drainage mill whenever I passed by.

Fire and vandalism have, though, claimed several of the Broads' finest windmills this century – notably the corn windmill at Thornham; the accidental fire which destroyed the smock mill at Wymondham; and the similar fate which removed forever the Mousehold Mill painted by Crome.

St Benet's Marsh Mill, close to Thurne, also caught fire at the turn of the century, resembling a giant Catherine wheel as showers of sparks from it swept across the river towards the village. Fortunately, the mill was not destroyed completely and was later restored by Ludham millwright Dan England.

Another of my favourites is the Sutton Windmill at Potter Heigham, which had the unique distinction of having its sails being struck by lightning, not once but twice: a story that seems to dispute the old saying that 'lightning never strikes twice'. It, too, has been restored to its former glory, and is claimed to be the largest windmill in England, as well as housing the Broads Museum, with its wonderful collection of historical artefacts.

I am glad that I had a chance to see some of the finest windmills of the Norfolk Broads before they

The converted Horning windmill.

Wisett post mill.

Burgh St Peter windmill.

disappeared – and to take photographs that capture something of their romance and beauty.

My love of exploring the Norfolk Broads also gave me the idea of recording details of the surviving watermills. It became something of a quest for me and my friend, Frances Procter, and we systematically set about finding the likely places where they might be found along our river valleys, and to photograph and sketch all those we could trace.

It was obvious when searching that watermills must stand astride a stream where there was a flow of water vigorous enough to turn a wheel. But Norfolk was comparatively flat, of course; therefore any enquiries would have to begin at the upper reaches. With this in mind, Frances and I consulted our maps and studied a book on the subject written in 1939 by the Reverend C.J.W. Messent, who recorded, sadly, that there were only 60 watermills still standing in the county. His book proved most useful, though, with plenty of information about their history.

It is thought that the Romans introduced watermills into Britain, and by the time of the Domesday Book of 1086, some 580 mills were listed in Norfolk and Suffolk, mostly of Saxon origin. Many of the present sites of watermills are probably the same as those – although the buildings have, of course, been successively renewed and improved.

During the Middle Ages, the lord of the manor, secular or ecclesiastic, who owned the mills, monopolised the milling industry and insisted that the people brought their corn to his mill to be ground.

Wrentham post mill.

Ludham windmill.

Tacolneston post mill.

Waxham Dyke.   *Potter Heigham.*

Above: *Cley windmill.*

Opposite: *'The Broadsman' – a sketch by Philippa Miller.*

Billingford – a landmark for airmen.

From time to time a mill – and the miller! – were sold as part of the estate. Later, the millers became tenants, or, if they were fortunate, owners, and the craft of milling was frequently handed down in the same family for generations.

For the next few centuries mills, providing the only source of power, were used not only for grinding corn but for many other purposes, such as making flock and paper, forging metal, sawing wood and irrigation.

It seems that various causes led to the decline of watermills. There were the ravages of the 'Black Death' and the Dissolution of the Monasteries, as well as fires and floods. Also, the increasing use of windmills and then, in the nineteenth century, the introduction of steam power, heralded their decline still further.

A century later and steel rollers were replacing millstones and even steam was giving way to diesel oil and electricity. In Norfolk, the great flood of 1912 and the impact of the two World Wars caused the closure of many country mills. These facts all made Frances and I realise our task would not be an easy one.

Left: *Denver Mill – a reminder of home for American bomber pilots.*

St Benet's Marsh Mill – a study in reflection.

We began our search for the remaining watermills in the very south of the county. There, under a little bridge just south of Lopham, was the source of not one but two rivers which formed the county boundary – the Ouse flowing westward to the Wash and the Waveney meandering until it reached the sea at Great Yarmouth.

After many outings – some as many as 40 miles from our base in Norwich – we acquired a fairly comprehensive record and found a number of picturesque and interesting places. Unfortunately, we found very few working watermills; most were silent and neglected, while there were just scanty traces of others. Thankfully, we were just in time in several instances.

By now we were completely hooked on the subject, and I produced a little book in verse, *In Search of Watermills*, illustrated with drawings and

Philippa Miller's cover design for her book, In Search of Windmills.

Left: *Sutton Windmill at Stalham, home to the Broads Museum.*

Below: *Diagram of the machinery in a watermill.*

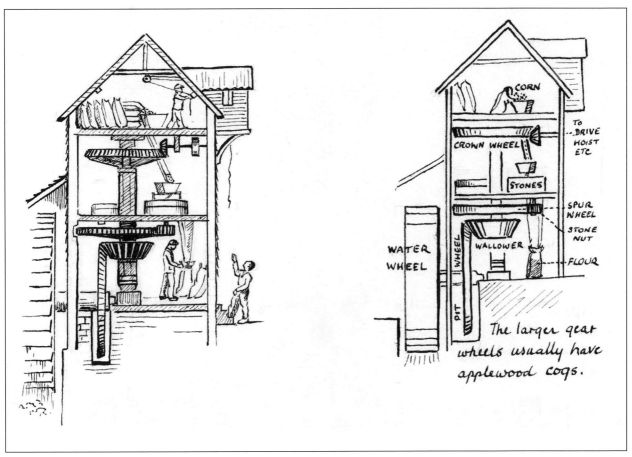

Oxnead Mill was once a flock and paper-making mill.

Stoke Holy Cross Mill on the River Tas, the original home of Colman's Mustard.

'Lakenham Mill' – a watercolour by Philippa Miller

Inset: *Sketch of Hardingham Mill, burned down for the film* The Shuttered Room.

Itteringham Mill has been restored, with a tea-garden for visitors.

photographs of all the mills we had located. It was very pleasing to find the Stoke Holy Cross Mill, where Colman's had first begun to make their name in mustard before moving to Carrow Road, in good order, but sad to learn the fate of the once fine building at Hardingham on the River Yare. This had been deliberately burned down in 1967 for the climax of a mystery film, *The Shuttered Room*, starring Carol Lynley and Gig Young – the story of which was supposed to be set in New England but was actually filmed in Cornwall and Hardingham!

Of all the mills we visited, Itteringham Mill particularly appealed to us as the owner, author and poet, Derek Neville, had opened a tea garden – just as my father had done all those years before – to help fund the upkeep of the mill. He became a good friend and the mill a favourite rendezvous for us.

Chapter 8
Signs of the Times

Many interesting aspects of the history of the Norfolk Broads are to be found illustrated on the village signs that have been appearing in ever-increasing numbers all over the district since the 1930s. The fact they were becoming so varied and original in their designs was one of the reasons that Frances Procter and I began to visit and photograph them. I was particularly interested in those which featured the subjects closest to my heart, like wherries, windmills and water pumps, and when we found that out of a total of over 300 in Norfolk, some 40 illustrated these evocative reminders of the past. In was clear to us that the people of Broadland were equally keen on acknowledging this part of their heritage.

The idea of having a decorated sign to indicate the presence of a village originated in Norfolk early in the twentieth century. In 1912, King George V erected some of the earliest village signs on the Royal Estate around Sandringham: at Wolferton – which became known as 'The King's Signpost' – Shernbourne and Flitcham. A few years later, in 1920, his son, the Duke of York (later King George VI), made a plea for the restoration of village signs while he was speaking at the opening of the Royal Academy.

An immediate interest was aroused in this art craft and soon other signs were being erected. The Broads can claim one of the earliest when Horning put up one on the main road between Wroxham and Potter Heigham. A report of the event in the *Eastern Daily Press* of 30 June 1927 explained that the sign had been erected by local subscription and was a clear indication that, 'Horning believes in publicity'. The article added a transcript of what had been inscribed on the sign:

'Beneath the centre panel is a shield of the arms of St Benet's Abbey, while below the shield is a tablet

'The King's Signpost' at Wolferton, erected by King George V.

Thomas de Sherborne on the village sign that bears his name.

'Blind Man's Gate' – a watercolour by Philippa Miller.

St Felix bringing Christianity to the district on the Flitcham sign.

One of the earliest signs on the Broads, at Potter Heigham.

Skating on the frozen Broads on the Welney village sign.

'The Pulham Pig' airship features at Pulham St.Mary.

setting forth arresting information about the abbey, the present abbot, the rood screen at Ransworth Church and Horning itself.'

The lead that Horning gave spread across the county, although subsequent village signs were less verbose and rather more attractively illustrative of local features. The Festival of Britain in 1951 gave a further impetus to the idea of this form of commemoration, and nowadays it is claimed that Norfolk is richer in village signs than any other county of England.

This is certainly largely due to the influence of the royal family and the handiwork of Henry R. Carter of Swaffham, a former art teacher of Swaffham, who has been responsible for designing and carving many of the signs. Mr Carter, a cousin of Howard Carter, the Egyptologist who discovered Tutankhamen's tomb, has created signs that are instantly recognisable as his work, and their number now runs into many dozens. Several local blacksmiths have also cleverly wrought those carved in metal.

The signs, mounted on a post at least six feet high, are usually set in a solid base. They often record the origin of a village name, some important event or character, or perhaps a local industry or major historical discovery. They have quickly become a focal point of the area and many show great variety and originality as well as history and even, on occasions, some humour.

An A-Z of Village Signs

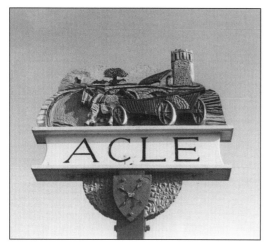

ACLE: *A windmill and a wherry feature on this market town's sign.*

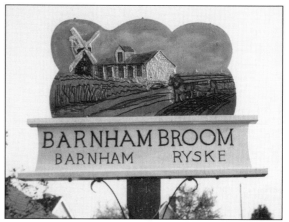

BARNHAM BROOM: *The wind- and water-mills have long disappeared.*

BARTON TURF: *Wrought-iron sign of a wherry for a Broads beauty spot.*

Above: BRUNDALL: *Commemorates boat building on the River Yare.*

Left: BURNHAM MARKET: *The mill has now been replaced by new houses.*

An A-Z of Village Signs

CANTLEY: *Wherries traded through the village bound for Norwich.*

CLIPPESBY: *A familiar windmill beside the River Bure.*

Left centre: DENVER: *Features the six-storey corn mill built in 1835.*
Left: DILHAM: *Wind- and water-mills complement a passing wherry*

An A-Z of Village Signs

EARSHAM: *A working watermill has been here since Saxon times.*

FORNCETT: *A post mill once stood on high ground in the parish.*

FREETHORPE: *One of many windmills that once served the area.*

GARBOLDISHAM: *A miniature post mill celebrates the famous original.*

GELDESTON: *A full-rigged wherry heads for the old maltings.*

Right: GRESHAM: *The village once boasted a post mill and mill house.*

An A-Z of Village Signs

HALVERGATE: *A stately heron observes an old drainage mill.*

HARDINGHAM: *The village was once dominated by a mill house.*

HINDRINGHAM: *A carved oak sign commemorates a long-lost windmill.*

HEMSBY: *A drainage mill maintained the ploughing land hereabouts.*

Right: MARTHAM: *A trading wherry passes a windmill en route to Yarmouth.*

An A-Z of Village Signs

RUNHAM: *A wherry navigates the ferry point at 'Runham Swim'.*

EAST RUSTON: *A charming metal sign of an old tower mill.*

SALHOUSE: *A trading boat sailing through the centre of the reed industry.*

Centre right: GREAT SNORING: *Former water mill mentioned in the Domesday Book.*

Right: WEST SOMERTON: *A 3D metal sign of wind pump, mill and wherry.*

An A-Z of Village Signs

SOUTHERY: *A windmill landmark familiar to passing wherries.*

SPROWSTON: *Artist John Crome's famous windmill on Mousehold.*

STALHAM: *A tempered steel wherry sign on the corn route to Yarmouth.*

SUTTON: *A building place for wherries and the site of a picturesque windmill.*

SURLINGHAM: *An iron sign marking the heyday of yachting on the Broads.*

SWAFIELD: *The core of a post mill supports an iron wherry.*

 An A-Z of Village Signs

THURLTON: *A corn mill minus its sails records a chapter of history.*

UPTON WITH FISHLEY: *Two villages offer a panorama of Broads life.*

WACTON: *A 195-foot high post mill operated here from 1675 to 1902.*

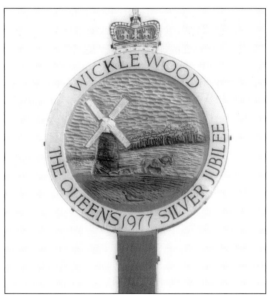

WICKLEWOOD: *A typical Broads windmill saluting a royal jubilee.*

WROXHAM: *Marking one of the largest boating centres on the Broads.*

There are some village signs painted in a true, robust peasant style, while others, in wood, are examples of fine art and craftsmanship. All convey a community spirit and a sense of belonging as well as stimulating a pride in the English way of life. Among two of the most unusual that Frances and I found were those at Welney and Pulham St Mary.

The Welney sign, which was made by Henry Carter, depicts two men skating on a frozen river past a windmill, and it immediately reminded me of my father and brother at Oulton Broad after it had been turned into an ice rink in the winter. Apparently, Welney Wash often became flooded and frozen and many skating races were held. Norwegian long skates were apparently introduced to England at Welney with speed rather than figure-skating the aim.

The sign at Pulham St Mary is very different and shows a huge airship, the R33, tethered to its mooring mast. The airship – which was sometimes jokingly referred to locally as 'The Pulham Pig' – was in a vast hangar near the railway at Pulham in 1919. It was said to be based on the design of a German Zeppelin that had been captured in 1916. The airship did not have an altogether trouble-free existence – being badly damaged while moored to its mast during a great gale on 16 August 1925 – although its sister ship, the R34, did fly successfully from England to America and back. The village sign was paid for by various communal efforts and was carved and painted by the aptly named Mr Wing, who was a sign-writer of note.

In fact, the growing popularity of the village sign has engendered a new form of 'folk art' of which Norfolk can be proud and which is rapidly spreading to other counties. I have been actively involved myself, designing the sign for the village of Starston, which was carved and painted by an artist friend, John Robinson. I even officiated at the opening ceremony at Happisburgh, which was indeed a very 'happy' occasion.

There has also grown up the hobby of 'village sign hunting', and I have been told that many people now enjoy searching out and photographing the signs when on holiday in Norfolk. I am sure there will be more created in the future, ensuring the continuation of this enjoyable pastime.

[Philippa Miller and Frances Proctor located, photographed and sketched over 300 village signs in Norfolk, publishing their findings in three books in the early seventies. The two authors were particularly proud when Queen Elizabeth and the Queen Mother accepted copies of the books for their libraries. The selection of 40 signs in the following pages focuses on those subjects which, as Philippa wrote, were 'closest to my heart'.]

'The Boom Towers' – the remains of the ancient city wall above Bishops Bridge erected in the time of Edward II – a watercolour by Philippa Miller.

Chapter 9
Memories of Norwich

Once, many years ago, I returned early one evening by train to Norwich from my home in Oulton Broad in order to join some friends who were having a little party. It was November and quite dark when I arrived – but I was not prepared for the impenetrable fog that I met as I left the station. It was to be an experience that would remain in my memory, all the more vivid as the events of one night were repeated almost every evening when war darkened our world.

At first I was with a crowd of fellow passengers heading for the city. But soon they dispersed and I groped my lonely way up Prince of Wales Road. There were no buses or taxis, of course, so I carried on walking. I hoped I'd know when I reached the crossroads, but I wasn't sure. Even the one other pedestrian I passed didn't know where he was.

However, after much weaving about, I arrived at Tombland. But there were now no friendly walls to feel and discover where I was. Later, I had to negotiate the open space at Stump Cross, where the roads diverged.

The crossing at Magdalen Gates was another hazard. When I finally came to the solid continuous wall along Sewell Park and the gates of the Blyth School playing-fields I was more than thankful.

But there was no one about anywhere. The visibility was literally nil. I have never known such a dense fog before or since. Now I had to cross the road and turn right. I might as well have been blindfolded.

However, in spite of being very tired and rather frightened, I reached my friend's gate. But I was not familiar with the garden layout. Could I find the path?

I ended up crawling on my knees and feeling the edges of the path – almost crying with exhaustion and frustration. I was late for the party by now and could hear the happy laughter indoors. But nobody heard me until I knocked frantically on the door.

When the door opened, the girls inside only needed one look to see what sort of state I was in. They gave me a hot drink and star treatment and I gradually began to feel a lot better.

Several hours later we all donned our winter things and ventured out again into the darkness. I need not have feared a repeat of my nightmare journey – outside, thankfully, lay a calm, moonlit, fog-free night!

To me – the girl from Oulton Broad – Norwich, with its compactness and central position in Norfolk, was a fascinating and exciting city replete with reminders of the past. Walking along the riverside, enjoying the charm of Pull's Ferry and Bishop's Bridge, or just observing the busy scenes along the wharves, I often use to marvel that this was a port, some 28 miles from the sea.

The main part of the city and the curving River Wensun is encircled by gentle hills, though both Ber Street and Mousehold Heath are of considerable height. Within the city walls there are numerous ancient buildings, medieval streets and courtyards, as well as intriguing alleyways that no visitor should miss.

The 'Boom Towers' on King Street are a particularly imposing illustration of the city's history. Conisford, or King Street Gates, stood at the point where the walls, descending from the height, had their natural termination. The visitor who follows the line of the wall to the river will discover above Bishops Bridge the remains of the towers erected with the walls in the time of Edward II.

For those who care to go wandering, it is only a short walk from the magnificent Norwich Cathedral down to the river at Pull's Ferry, or alternatively to the Castle or St Peter Mancroft near the central market place. Ever since I was a child, a visit to this market to see the stalls, with gay tilts above them and the colourful arrangements of flowers, fruit and vegetables, has been a never-failing delight.

There are parks and gardens throughout Norwich that have also excelled themselves in creating colourful floral displays and providing amenities for local people to walk in and enjoy. Earlham, Eaton, Waterloo and Chapelfield have all offered countless thousands of local people many happy hours of relaxation – and in my case scenes that have inspired me to sketch and paint.

Mousehold, an area of natural heath and woodland, was given to the people of Norwich long ago. It

Some of the shops in picturesque Elm Hill.

The busy thoroughfare of Duke Street.

is a delightful and breezy place to explore. From up here, overlooking the city, it is possible see what a fascinating blend of the medieval and the modern Norwich has become – and why it provided a constant source of inspiration for my camera and my brush.

Once there were five cinemas and two theatres in Norwich. Over the years, the unique Maddermarket Theatre, developed by Nugent Monck, has put on all Shakespeare's plays, as well as many other famous productions. The acting, directing, costumes and scenery are invariably excellent, in spite of the small and intimate setting of the Tudor stage, and the players are all local people, not paid artists.

The 'Spring Gardens', on the riverbank opposite Thorpe Station, are an environment not to be missed. I remember the trees hung with coloured lights illuminating the grassy walks. Incidentally, there were two other stations at that time.

The City Hall, the ancient Guild Hall, the Assembly House, the Theatre Royal and at least three churches were all within a stone's throw of each other. I once heard it said that Norwich possessed a

church for each Sunday and a pub for every day of the year.

A girl's school occupied the Assembly House when I first knew it. Later, it became a meeting-place for the citizens of Norwich, where they could enjoy concerts, exhibitions and refreshments. St Andrew's Hall became the venue for much larger functions, such as orchestral concerts, antique fairs and the like. It was also where the Blythe School, at which I became a teacher, held their prize-giving days and Christmas parties.

When I first came to Norwich in 1928 there were still trams encircling the centre and radiating on routes in all directions. But they were not much used by me, for living near the centre I was within easy reach of most things quite easily. Later, when I migrated northwards to live near the Blythe School, a bicycle was all I needed.

I recall, too, that for a long time Norwich possessed a special feature. Practically in the centre, on the plain below the Castle, was the site of a weekly cattle market. Cows, sheep and pigs were all brought there from the countryside to be sold. The market was a great attraction to one and all – especially at Easter. Then the scene was transformed into a busy,

Cathedral Close, leading to Norwich Cathedral.

The unmistakable spire of Norwich's fine cathedral by day (right)...

... and by night.

'The Cloisters of Norwich Cathedral' – a watercolour by Philippa Miller.

noisy, colourful venue of swings, coconut shies, whirling roundabouts and all the lights and organs of the fairground. Even then it was a relic of the past and referred to as the 'Tombland Fair'.

Memories like these and many more confirmed in me the opinion then – as it does today – that Norwich is a very fine city indeed.

Pulls Ferry, which I mentioned earlier, was close to where I first lived in the GFS Hostel, a large, three-storey brick building in Cathedral Close opposite the south transept of Norwich Cathedral. The Ferry is a fifteenth-century Watergate situated on the bank of the Wensun just below the close and derives its name from a certain John Pull, who ran both an inn and the ferry there from 1796 to 1841. In medieval times, a canal was made from this ferry to the site of Norwich Cathedral in order to transport building materials, including limestone, from Caen in France, to construct the great edifice.

It was here, one August, that my art student friend, Peggy Haes and I had what must have seemed like a hare-brained idea to anyone else. We were going to paddle from Pulls Ferry to Oulton Broad in my tiny canoe. The craft was just 11 feet long, with two tiny decks fore and aft, and there was just about enough room for both of us: one at each end sitting cross-legged with a small pile of necessities in the middle.

When Peggy arrived late on the afternoon we had chosen for our adventure, she surveyed what must have looked like an impossible situation, but said nothing and squeezed into the canoe. I knew in that moment she was a good pal to have for the expedition.

As it turned out, we could not have chosen two days of worse weather if we had tried. But it was a glorious evening as we left and we began the journey happily enough once we had learned the art of balancing. We ignored the stares of the locals as we paddled by – not for the world would we have allowed ourselves to appear cramped or amateurish – and settled down to paddle briskly with the tide.

Yachts, launches and huge trading vessels passed us by with various comments from those on board – mostly audible and not very complimentary. When we needed a rest we moored loosely to any convenient stump or clump of reeds. But getting into or out of the canoe proved a tricky business with only two inches of freeboard!

The wash of motorboats nearly swamped us on several occasions, but Peggy bailed out determinedly. By the end of the trip she said she would be able to pass the stiffest examination in the subject and now knew why she had been asked to come.

After several hours of paddling, and darkness having fallen, we reached Bramerton, where I proposed we should put up for the night. We hauled the canoe out of the water, arranged all our things and erected a tarpaulin. Then we gathered some brushwood, lit a fire and cooked some sausages, which we ate while admiring the mirrored world all around us. Then we slept the sleep of the exhausted.

Almost as soon as it was light we started out on our second day. The rain started, too. But all we could do was shrug our shoulders, eat our breakfast as best we could, don our macs and get going, hoping the skies would clear. Before the trip, I had painted the paddles a bright orange, perhaps sensing we might need cheering up at some point. I was not wrong.

The rain continued to beat down. We even tried to sketch at our next stop and, if I say so myself, they were actually not bad water-colours. We eventually reached Brundall and sat in a shed for a while to dry off before going shopping. At least we were suitably clad, in our macs with towels as scarves and bathing caps on our heads. What a sight we must have looked!

Then we paddled on towards Reedham and Cantley. Here the river is very wide and the tide was strong. Gone were the sheltered reaches lined with willows. We had to paddle close to tall banks of waving reeds, their feathery tops high above us.

The day became blustery and cold again, not to

Norwich Market in full swing.

mention wet. It seemed so ridiculous, as this was supposed to be the height of summer! We were soaking again, but determined, and suddenly just burst out laughing at ourselves until we ached.

Then came one of those miraculous changes that can occur on the Broads. The skies cleared, the wind dropped and everything was bathed in a golden light. We pulled up in the shelter of an old mill, dried off, girded our loins, so to speak, and set off again in good heart.

Time didn't matter to us. Nothing mattered except that we were messing about in a boat and having such fun. What did we care when two launches passed by leaving jeering remarks from the male passengers on the air? What did it matter that we had to bail out frequently and put up with the rain cascading down our necks as the reeds bent over in the wind?

Our next stop for the night was at Langley. Here we hauled the canoe out of the water and slept in it like sardines, with the tarpaulin stretched across everything. When one of us turned over the other had to do the same out of necessity!

Again, the next morning, we made an early start and paddled hard to reach Cantley in time for lunch. The only thing was, the inhabitants said we were so early they called it breakfast! This, though, gave us

plenty of time to do the last few miles. Indeed, we even took advantage of some wind to 'sail' through the final three miles, with Peggy holding up the tarpaulin while I steered.

Why our final arrival at Oulton Broad after those 28 demanding and adventurous miles was not heralded by a brass band I shall never know. In fact, my brother, Martin, came to meet us with a motor launch and cheekily offered to tow us to Miller's Boatyard. But after all of those miles of hard work behind us, we simultaneously gave him the sharp rejoinder, 'No thank you very much!'

This canoe trip did nothing to dampen my enthusiasm for trips on the Broads and I later had a very wind-blown weekend with another friend, Pamela Baker, when we hired a yacht, the *Whippet*, at Wroxham. Using the earlier skills I had acquired, we bravely set out and sailed – once again in wind and rain – to Salhouse Broad, where we spent our first night.

The next morning we headed for Ranworth, negotiating the long dyke successfully, and explored the Broad, intrigued by a heron patiently waiting for a likely fish below his perch.

We returned to the main river and headed eastward with a steady wind at our backs – which entailed frequent gybes all the way to Thurne Mouth.

117

King Street.

The Cattle Market.

Then, turning north and east, we sailed along Heigham Sound, enjoying the wonderful light effects on the water.

As we reached Horsey Mere, the wind became a real gale and we found ourselves almost nose-diving with each gust as we crossed open water. Obviously we had to lower sail, which poor Pam, a complete novice, undertook while I endeavoured to steer, not daring to turn into the wind at such a speed. Thankfully, we arrived in the dyke safely and managed to moor – but it had all been more than we bargained for and not a little scary.

The following day the wind was not so strong and we negotiated the River Ant in order to reach Barton

118

Broad, a lovely stretch with reedy islands and sheltered nooks. The dyke to Neatishead was a haven from the wind and here we were visited by swans still with tiny bits of grey fluff riding on their mother's back. Our shattered nerves began to recover at this delightful scene.

Afterwards we felt that *Whippet* had been a very suitable name for our ship on such a strenuous adventure. It ended, though, would you believe, in complete calm on a golden evening. So calm, in fact, that we had to ask for a tow back to base by some friendly folk who happened to pass by in their cruiser!

I joined the Blythe Secondary School in Norwich in January 1930 as a teacher of arts and crafts after completing my training at the Lowestoft School of Art and obtaining the Secondary Teachers' Drawing Certificate. It was to be my one and only appointment in a career that lasted until I retired in 1965.

Up until the Second World War, it was customary for our staff to wear their gowns, which of course not only indicated their university status, but also added a certain amount of authority and dignity to their position. The girls wore the school's uniform: blouses, jerseys in winter, gymslips, panama hats in summer and berets in winter. They also wore blazers, black with red borders, which made them all look very smart on occasions such as speech and field days.

The classrooms were designed so that the inner sides in each of the two quadrangles could open on to the corridors, thus providing fresh air and access to the grass and gravel paths surrounding the central features, one a sundial, the other a bird bath with a thatched roof.

North of the main building was the Grey House, reorganised into dining rooms, kitchen and libraries, and beyond that the tennis courts and hockey pitches, as well as the games pavilion. Just outside the art and craft rooms was the asphalt playground, with a grassy dell with cycle sheds beyond the Grey House. This grand plan of open classrooms that was probably very healthy for the young – especially in summer – was somewhat of a trial in bitter weather. But we seemed to survive!

At least we could escape the staff-room if we were free. Our colleagues were a united and friendly group, which was just as well, as the room was not very large but had to contain desks, shelves and chairs for some 40 or so teachers. Yet I never remember any bickering or backbiting – due partly, I think, to the personality and kindly authority of the Head, Mrs F.E. Whitaker. The room was certainly crowded when a full staff meeting was called, though!

Sometimes when a pupil knocked on the staff-room door and asked to speak to 'Miss Miller', for

Historic St John Maddermarket.

instance, this could cause a smile – as there were two Miss Millers! One of the staff wrote an amusing little song on the subject, plagiarising the song 'Titwillow', which was duly acted out at one of the annual staff entertainments provided for the girls.

The central hall, used for morning assemblies and the short daily service, was also used for school plays, and there was great variety in the subjects offered each year and performed by the girls. The school had acquired a set of 'flats' – steps and boxes to be utilised in these productions – which, together with curtains, gave the staff, especially the other Miss Miller, who was the producer, and myself, opportunities to use our ingenuity over 30 years and more.

We were expected to provide Tudor interiors, woodland glades, prisons or tepees, garden stair-

A play produced at the Maddermarket in 1926.

Pulls Ferry, Norwich.

'Fye Bridge' – a watercolour by Philippa Miller, c.1925.

ways and balconies and many other settings for the young actresses playing all manner of roles, such as Lady Jane Grey, St Joan, Hiawatha, The Blue Bird, Henry VIII, St Simon Stylites, Lady Precious Stream and more whose names I have now forgotten.

Over the years, the staff performed a number of frivolous sketches and short plays for the amusement of the girls. I especially remember *Dick Whittington*, written by Pamela Baker, in which almost all of the staff took part and we had a hilarious time. Sometimes a number of mistresses would act the part of a rather brainless class. Once in an 'English Lesson', a supposed country girl put up her hand and, when told to speak, gabbled, 'Oi shew them

sen'ences we dunter moi mum an she say why dun't we taak praaper?'

Then there was the occasion when the tables were turned and the senior girls cleverly picked out some of the little habitual foibles of the staff. They wandered about the stage mimicking them so cleverly that most of us recognised our colleagues and were hard pressed not to laugh even louder than the rest of the audience.

The domestic staff produced a great array of excellent costumes for all of these productions, while my class and I set about making all the props required, such as swords and flowers, lanterns or lions, even banks and cauldrons.

A trader on its way from Norwich to Yarmouth.

From Norwich to Lowestoft by canoe!

'Riverbank at Bramerton' – a watercolour by Philippa Miller.

Sheltering from a gale in the Whippet.

In one production we needed a dog to bark at an appointed moment. The animal had to be heard but not seen – and we had no means of recording a bark in those days. On another occasion the dog had to wander across the stage searching for something. My own black poodle, 'Puck', solved both problems. No one knew that I was also wandering across the stage at the same time – concealed behind the back scenery.

When not in use, all the larger sets had to be stored elsewhere. The task of superintending the job fell to me, and it was no mean feat to store everything high up in the dark loft of the girl's cycle shed. This was believed to have been the barn where Black Beauty was stabled in Anna Sewell's classic story. Outside it stood a beech tree that the authoress had planted. Later, the shed became well known as the Sewell Barn Theatre.

Since I retired, I have regularly been asked what life was like in an all-girl school in those days. From some of the comments I received after describing my experiences, I realised that things had changed in the classroom and thought I should write down the details of an average day.

Teaching arts and crafts is, in a sense, a repetitive job, but always there were different, amusing or amazing things happening – problems with the girls or their work, or duties required in the running of the school. There was one year, for example, when the School Examinations were in progress that I had to go out suddenly at 7a.m. to find and pick enough thistles for a nature drawing exam due to start at 9a.m.

When I first began teaching in the thirties, staff usually had one free afternoon a week. No one can believe that now. Later, you were lucky to get one free period per day. On top of schoolwork, there was always one's own subject to study and practise in order to keep up with current trends.

A typical day would begin with me arriving in time to prepare the necessary equipment for my lessons. Then I would go down to the staff-room to see if there were any notices concerning school events. After morning assembly at 8.50a.m., I would return to the art or craft room to await the appearance of perhaps 30 young first-formers.

Information, instruction and materials were given out and the class might begin an exercise in penman-

Blythe School in 1929.

Staff in gowns hurrying to lessons.

ship with an eye to future lessons on manuscript writing – a subject that was then sometimes taken in the School Certificate Examination. Our 11-year-olds were set to create border patterns, using a variety of strokes, thin and thick, straight or curved, and usually in one or two colours. Thirty minutes later, all would have to be cleared up and stored ready for marking and comments.

Another, older, group might be next to arrive for a double period. Homework would be collected and reviewed. Then the girls would settle down to draw a spray of flowers or, alternatively, begin sketching a still-life study, eventually to be painted in watercolours.

After lunch, more girls would come to me for their afternoon lessons in art or craft. This period

'Memories of Some Lessons' – a sketch by Philippa Miller.

The Blythe School quadrangle.

Hard at work in the Craft Room.

The staff room at Blythe School.

The impressive games pavilion.

Top and above: *The annual field day in 1930.*

The Blythe School production of Henry VIII *(1936).*

Staff of Blythe School in Dick Whittington *(1948).*

Teachers impersonating girls in a Blythe School concert.

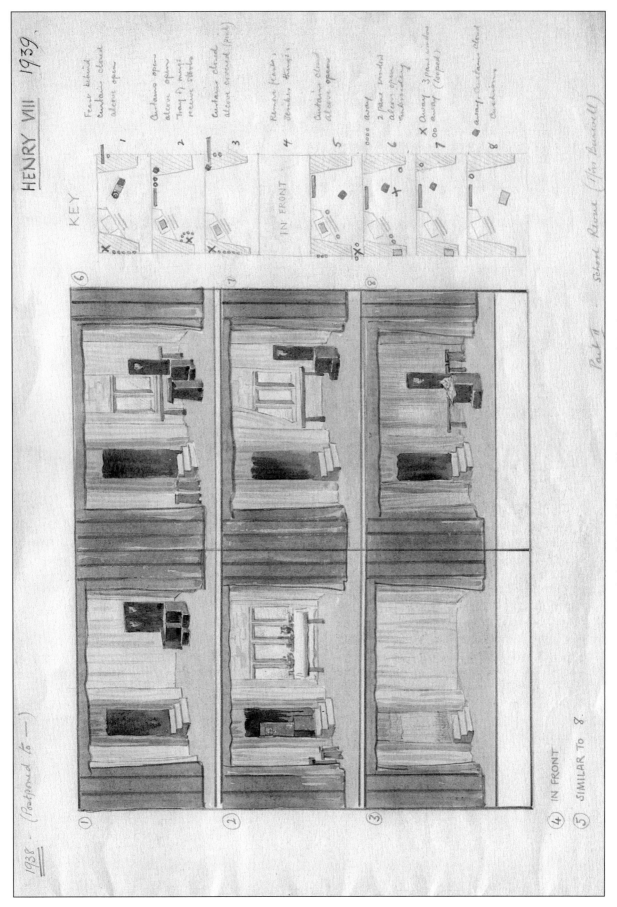

A sketch by Philippa Miller for Henry VIII (1939).

'Lady Precious Stream' – a sketch by Philippa Miller (1960).

might be devoted to the subject of design for a patterned material that was going to be printed – or might even be carried out using lino blocks or stencilling.

One of my lessons might be about repeating a floral motif – a half-drop arrangement – but in the drawing the spray was to be ignored and only the background coloured in, then the flowers embellished slightly. The idea was to show that space can be as important as the motif itself. A popular idea with the juniors and middle-school pupils was the creation of a tartan pattern by ruling many coloured lines. It certainly encouraged accuracy!

As far as the staff themselves were concerned, meetings would sometimes be held by the headmistress during the mid-morning coffee break. There was a welcome cup of tea at ten past three, which was always especially welcome after supervision duty in the lunch hour.

In class, time had to be found to comment on girls' achievements, the encouragement of individual pupils and sometimes dealing with less pleasant aspects of behaviour. I have to say that this was comparatively rare in the years I taught, thanks be.

All in all, though, I can certainly say that I enjoyed my school career. The days were full, often tiring, sometimes worrying, but on the whole very satisfying.

Chapter 10
Bombs over the Broads

In 1939, school and home life was proceeding almost normally for me, but Adolf Hitler was lording it over Europe and becoming a greater and greater threat. The Prime Minister, Neville Chamberlain, tried unsuccessfully to obtain 'Peace in our time', but the nation had now been warned and various preparations were being put in place.

Most of us on the staff of the Blythe School attended classes in anti-gas training and first aid months before the declaration of war. In July 1938 I learned all about the hated 'gas masks' that had been issued from the Red Cross and how they were to be used in the event of a raid. We were informed that

local pharmacists would act as 'Gas Detector Officers' and a 'rattling sound' would warn us of a gas attack. The children were given instructions in how to put the masks on and we were all ordered to carry them in their little boxes at all times.

The following March, along with several of my colleagues, I qualified in first aid. We were all given leaflets about how to deal with everything, from what to do after an attack to treating burns, with the firm admonition that the piece of paper had to be kept in your pocket or handbag at all times.

Some of the teachers also attended fire-fighting sessions and were initiated into the methods that

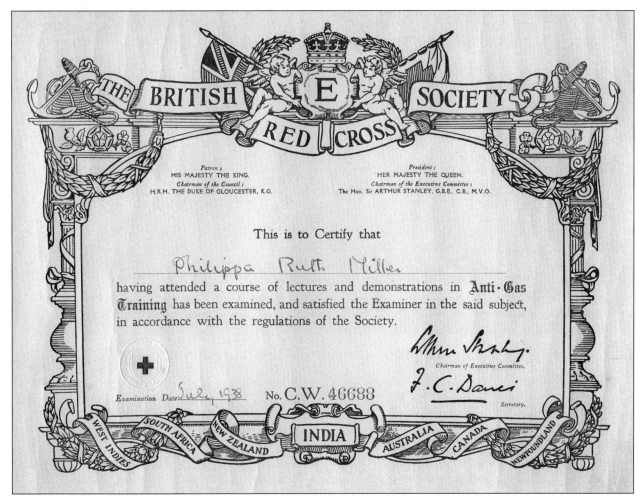

Citizens such as the author were prepared for any poison gas attacks by the Germans.

'Moonlight Devastation' - a unique watercolour of Norwich at war by Philippa Miller.

were to be used. My most vivid memory of this time was when a few of us and our fairly portly and asthmatic headmistress went down to a place in Baker Street, Norwich, where there was a small corrugated shed in which we had to practise putting out a fire burning fiercely in the middle of the room. While wearing our gas masks, and with stirrup pumps at the ready, we were expected to crawl on all fours and approach the seat of the fire and direct our hoses upon it. A reasonably efficient team effort defeated the flames. I was extremely impressed by our plucky HM literally 'getting down to it'!

During the summer holidays, the digging of trenches for air-raid shelters was hastily begun along both sides of the school. They were to be concrete lined with steps at each end. But by the beginning of term – and just before the war started – they were not yet finished. So all but the senior girls were told to

Issued by the Ministry of Health and the Department of Health for Scotland.

FIRST AID IN BRIEF

Read this carefully several times, then carry it in your pocket or bag

AFTER AN AIR ATTACK First Aid Parties will reach the wounded within a few minutes. Even such a short time counts. The man or woman on the spot can save lives by immediate and proper action.

Be prepared to see severe wounds. Be courageous and keep your head. Keep your mind on your duty to your injured fellow man.

Everyone in these days of danger should carry several clean handkerchiefs or small towels. These can be used as bandages, and their inner laundered surfaces are quite suitable for application to open wounds as a first dressing.

Unless a patient is in a highly dangerous place you should treat him where he lies. To lift or drag the wounded can do serious damage. Your general rule is that the moving and transport should be left to trained parties.

The first and most important duty of the civilian helper who first reaches a casualty is to stop bleeding.

When you cut a thumb you naturally grab it firmly with the fingers of your other hand. That application of pressure to a bleeding wound is the correct thing to do in all cases.

TO STOP BLEEDING

Press on the bleeding point with fingers or hands. As soon as possible apply a clean thick pad of folded handkerchief or towel. Use an inner surface of your handkerchiefs or towels. Keep up the pressure through this pad. Bandage the pad firmly in position over the wound. Be sure that the dressing is applied firmly enough to control the loss of blood. If there is still oozing of blood past or through the pad renew pressure over the whole dressing.

BLEEDING FROM ARM OR LEG

Press on the wound with fingers or hands. Apply a clean thick pad as soon as possible. Keep up pressure through the pad. Bandage the pad firmly over the wound. If this fails, pass a bandage, tie, handkerchief, elastic or fabric belt, or similar article, round the limb as close t... at a point between the wound and the trunk. Kno... limb is loosely encircled. Pass a stick through the s... the tightening of the band round the limb stops the... not to pinch the skin. Hold tight till the First Aid... have to do this, make a note of the time when you ti... it to the patient or attach it to the limb. It is v... hospital surgeon should know this.

PRACTISE PUTTING ON YOUR RESPIRATOR

1. Hold your breath. (*To inhale gas may be fatal.*) 2. Hold mask in front of face, thumbs inside straps. 3. Thrust chin well forward into mask. Pull straps as far over head as they will go. 4. Run finger round face-piece taking care head-straps are not twisted.

MAKE SURE IT FITS

See that the rubber fits snugly at sides of jaw and under chin. The head-straps should be adjusted so that they hold the mask firmly on the face. To test for fit, hold a piece of soft, flat rubber or of soft tissue paper to end of mask and breathe in. The rubber or paper should stick.

Arrows indicate points needing particular attention.

YOUR RESPIRATOR

COMPLETELY PROTECTS YOUR EYES, NOSE, THROAT AND LUNGS AGAINST ALL WAR GASES

ALWAYS KEEP YOUR RESPIRATOR SAFE, CLEAN AND EFFICIENT

IF YOU SUSPECT GAS, AT ONCE PUT ON YOUR RESPIRATOR AND GET UNDER COVER

F/48. (3167/1347.) Wt. 1633. 200M. 8/42. A., P. & S., Ltd. 428.   34—9999

Above: Rare leaflet containing information about first aid to be used after an air attack.

Above right: The people of Norwich were familiar with gas masks even before war broke out.

Right: Double honour for the local 'Wailing Winnies'.

THE LAST SIREN

Lowestoft Claims it, and Probably the First

Lowestoft is claiming that it had the last, and probably the first, air raid warnings in England. There may be some doubt about the first, because the warnings were general along the coast shortly after the official announcement at 11 a.m. on September 3rd, 1939, that war had been declared on Germany, and there was one in London. But there is not much doubt about the claim to the last, which was on Monday, when the siren sounded at 1.25, and the "all-clear" five minutes later. Unidentified aircraft approaching the coast turned out to be Allied planes.

Vickers medium tanks on exercises near Oulton Broad.

stay at home – except to come in once a week for a short time to collect work to do.

As a temporary measure, the senior cloakroom was turned into an air-raid shelter. When the trenches were finally completed all round the building, the girls were drilled to go in an orderly fashion from their classrooms down to their allotted trench when the alert – a siren – was sounded.

This warning actually wailed miserably the very first time. Soon, though, the noise of 'Wailing Winnie' – as the siren was called – became an almost everyday occurrence as we all got used to life underground…

I can remember very clearly that awful sinking feeling, on 3 September 1939, when it was announced that we were at war. First came a stunned silence, and all kinds of thoughts and fears began whirling through everyone's mind. Then, with a shrug, life went on!

The first siren warning by 'Wailing Winnie' was actually a false alarm, but it created quite an interest in the press, as it was later claimed that the Lowestoft district had the first and last siren calls of the war. Notwithstanding this, all went as planned with the drills and we soon became accustomed to filing 'down below'. The appropriate teacher for the lesson-to-come would then appear and endeavour to carry on in those very strange surroundings. If the warning was still in force at mealtime, the staff brought down lunch.

After a while, we realised that these alerts did not always herald an immediate raid and so we entered the period of time that became known as the 'Phoney War'. The only evidence we were at war was the sight and noise of tanks lumbering along the country roads or open countryside during exercises. I encountered a pair of Vickers Medium Tanks, Mark 1, speeding along land near Oulton Broad and took some photographs – although I was not sure I was breaking the law by doing so. The tanks, with their quick-firing turret gun and two machine guns in the hull sides, looked pretty fearsome to me and I felt comforted we had such machinery to repel an invasion.

Because of this threat, the government decided there were to be no more holidays for yachtsmen and sailors on Oulton Broad – or even outings to the seaside, for that matter. A two-mile exclusion zone for all visitors was imposed right around the coast. This sadly brought an end to my father's previously flourishing business.

There was nothing much untoward going on at school and we only retreated underground after the 'crash' warning. We all got used to carrying identity cards and, after instructions from the Norwich City Police under the 'Surrender of Firearms Act', I

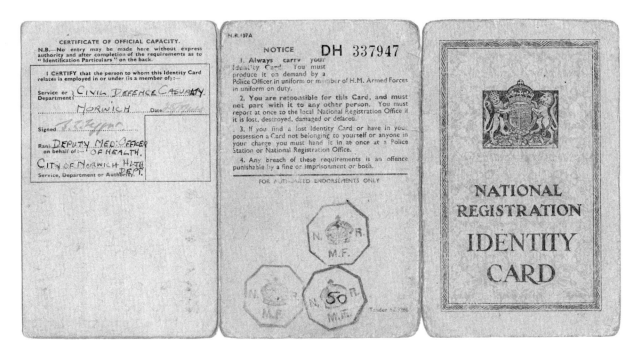

The author's identity card, which had to be carried at all times!

thought it best to hand in my revolver – although it was actually only an imitation!

Eventually, of course, things hotted up when raids on East Anglia by the Germans really began to build up. Norwich had its first air raid on 9 July 1940, when two German planes flew overhead. However, the sirens for once did not sound and the aircraft were able to drop their bombs on Carrow Road, killing and seriously injuring quite a number of factory girls. It seemed all the more of a tragedy because of the failure of the warning system.

After any raid, members of staff who were not in charge of forms would check to see that all were safely underground and then report back to the head-mistress. I remember one occasion when the mistress in charge of the trench said, 'Now, girls, those with 'Sou'westers' [rain proof hats] sit under the drips and those with 'Wellingtons' [rubber boots] go where the puddles are.' Then she began her French lesson! Another occasion was not so funny. Two of the staff were almost caught in a hail of bullets as they hurried down the steps of a trench.

I had an Anderson air-raid shelter in my garden into which I could descend for safety whenever 'Wailing Winnie' sounded while I was at home – which seemed almost every night. The Blackout was rigorously imposed on homes and vehicles, and every house had its windows criss-crossed with sticky tape to prevent those inside being injured by flying glass if a bomb fell in the vicinity.

We soon became used to hearing the drone of enemy planes, seeing the ring of flares light up the barrage balloons tethered overhead, and searchlights

trying to pinpoint the bombers for our ack-ack guns. We not only heard but also felt the crunch of high explosives as they fell in and around Norwich – the shattering thuds repeated over and over again. Then would come the 'All Clear!' – a continuous note on the siren and a blessed opportunity for some sleep before another anxious day.

During this time, my mother, Susan, continued to play an active part in Oulton Broad as organist and choirmaster at St Michael's, as well as making me welcome at weekend. She produced a variety of musical events, despite the constant threat of disruption. Once, during a Sunday service, she told me, the crash of bombs followed an alert while the rector was giving his sermon. He paused and said, 'No one will mind if you would like to shelter beneath the seats.' But apparently no one did!

My mother also felt an urge to record the events of the war she witnessed around Oulton Broad, especially because of its liability to attack from the Germans. Our coast had been considered vulnerable even in the time of Elizabeth I because the north shore shelves rapidly and large ships can approach closely. It was then, apparently, that the phrase was coined, 'He that would old England win, must at Weybourne Hope begin.' It was to be a source of satisfaction that Hitler obviously didn't know that.

As well as drawing the balloon barrage over our home, she sketched several squadrons of our aircraft flying overhead on their dangerous missions, and the moment two German airmen who had been shot down landed by parachute near Lowestoft. She also drew a 'sniper's nest' that had been built in a tree in preparation for any invaders – the

NORWICH CITY POLICE.

OUR REFERENCE

YOUR REFERENCE

CITY HALL,

NORWICH.

ALL OFFICIAL COMMUNICATIONS
TO BE ADDRESSED TO
" THE CHIEF CONSTABLE."
TELEPHONE 4040·3.

18th. June, 1940.

FIREARMS ACT, 1937.

Surrender of Firearms.

Received from   Miss Phillippa Miller,

of   34, Patricia Road,

Norwich.

the following described firearm(s) and ammunition
(if any) :-

Imitation revolver.

Number of Firearm Certificate cancelled:-   Nil

Chief Constable.

I, Phillipa Miller, hereby abandon all right to the above
d scribed firearm
Signed.........................Date......

Even an imitation revolver had to be surrendered in wartime!

whereabouts of which was probably supposed to be a secret.

Susan recorded the building of pillboxes and tank traps around the Broads at places like Ringland Bridge, and the erection of a scaffolding barrier and concrete blocks to stop enemy vehicles. Other types of tank traps were also going up at this time around the coast, as well as the strange-looking Alan-Williams steel turret, which had been designed for use with most weapons (Brancaster and Salthouse).

Some of the pillboxes in our area had been built for defence in the First World War. They were round,

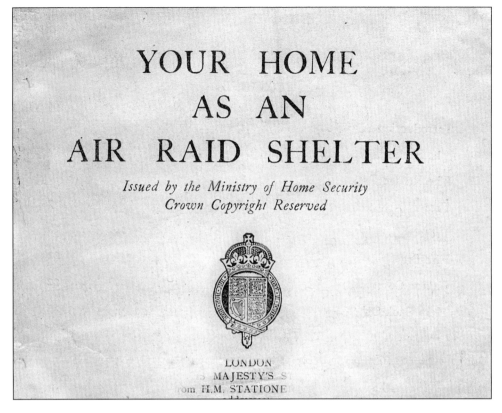

ILLUSTRATION 9.—ANOTHER IDEA FOR PROTECTING A WINDOW, USING TWO OLD DOORS AND SOME OLD PAINT CANS TO SUPPORT THE EARTH. THE OLD LINOLEUM IS TO PROTECT THE EARTH FROM SOAKING AND WASHING AWAY BY RAIN.

Top and above: Air-raid shelters saved the lives of many people in Norwich when bombs fell.

and hence the name, but later versions were hexagonal. The early ones were made of solid blocks, whereas the later hexagonal ones were of reinforced concrete and were sited at strategic points by roads (Oulton and Beccles), as well as along the coast where they were blatantly obvious, standing alone on a beach or cliff top (Lowestoft, Corton and Yarmouth). Some, like the pillbox at Killing Heath, had a spigot

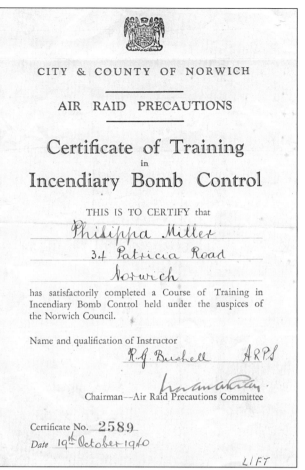

CITY & COUNTY OF NORWICH

AIR RAID PRECAUTIONS

Certificate of Training
in
Incendiary Bomb Control

THIS IS TO CERTIFY that

Philippa Miller

34 Patricia Road

Norwich

has satisfactorily completed a Course of Training in Incendiary Bomb Control held under the auspices of the Norwich Council.

Name and qualification of Instructor

R.G. Bushell ARPS

Chairman—Air Raid Precautions Committee

Certificate No. 2589

Date 19th October 1940

All ready for action – complete with certificate – but still a little nervous!

Oulton Broad searchlight crew waiting for action

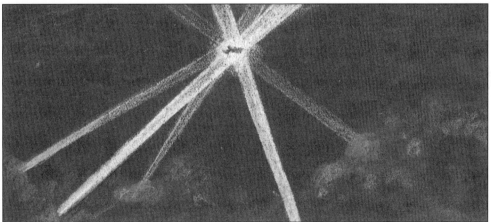

'Searchlights Over The Skies of the Broads' - sketches made at the height of the German attacks by Philippa Miller.

mortar base on which the Home Guard could mount their 'Blacker Bombard', which was capable of knocking out a tank. (I later painted this pillbox when nature had flourished amid the ruins, although nothing could quite hide its hostile purpose.)

Some of these pillboxes were disguised in ingenious ways. My mother recorded several of them; including a relic from the First World War at St Olaves which had an office built above it and served as a yacht station. And there were the latest versions that were made to look like a coal bunker, a clump of bushes, a 'milk bar' and even a holiday chalet.

However, because pillboxes were built in haste when war threatened, amateur efforts at reading instructions sometimes went awry, and a number were even erected facing the wrong way. A couple were even constructed on the coast below the high-water mark.

A neighbour of my mother told me that the pillboxes were manned by four men – each was given four bullets and told, 'This is your last line of defence – use your bullets and then give your life for your country.' The man in question was actually issued with a pike!

'Balloon Barrage Over Oulton Broad' – one of a series of sketches made by Susan Miller.

After the war, I decided to follow up my mother's interest in pillboxes as they were, after all, of historical significance to our area. With a friend, Joan Brooke, we found dozens of them all over Norfolk – some cleverly camouflaged, others buried in foliage and practically invisible – but all having resisted the harshest weather and even the efforts of Army disposal units to blow them up. A few had even tumbled onto beaches and were being relentlessly attacked by the waves (Happisburgh).

In fact, a number of our discoveries were quite unknown until then. A prize example being one I spotted due to a stinging nettle growing some five feet above ground level! As a result we contributed the information we had gathered about the constructions to the definitive study, *Pillboxes: A Study of UK Defences, 1940* by Henry Wills, which was published in 1985.

In one of the boxes, Joan and I found a few inscribed lines that seemed to serve as the perfect epitaph to these curious but worthy constructions. On an inside wall was written, 'Hitler has taken Poland, Holland, Belgium and France – but he will never take this Pill Box!' it was signed, 'J. Smith, Corporal, Home Guard'.

On the nights of 27–29 April 1942, Norwich was well and truly bombed in a series of attacks that became known as the 'Baedeker Raids'. They killed 321 people, injured 689 and did a vast amount of damage to different parts of the city, including our school, which suffered a direct hit. This completely destroyed the gymnasium, a building that stood on its own, and also shattered part of the roof of the cookery room. All the glass in the northern end of the building was blown out and even the door locks away at the other end of the school were damaged by the blast.

The staff had for some time taken turns in pairs to patrol the grounds at night on fire-watching duty. It was the quick thinking of Mr Hufton, the caretaker, which saved two lives one night. He was a veteran of the First World War and knew all the signs when a raid was on. He shouted orders just in time to the staff on duty to 'Get Down!'.

After the bomb that hit the school had done its worst, the staff assembled the following morning. It was sunny, but with a biting wind, which did not help as we tried to clear up all the debris, the dust and splintered glass. Sharp slivers had even got into the girls' desks and the contents of each one had to be removed in order that they could be searched. Everyone got tired of the almost permanent crunching noise of broken glass that was being swept up. It seemed to go on for hours – after which we rested, flat out, beside the Central Hall, revelling in the sun and sheltered from the wind.

The headmistress would anxiously count her staff and girls each time after raids. Thankfully, we had only one casualty in the whole war directly affecting the school [Brenda Waters, aged 17]. Admittedly, there was one morning after many disturbed nights when a member of staff did not appear. But a search revealed that she had only overslept.

Another memory from that time was the day of the rumour that there was an unexploded bomb on

The RAF takes the war to Hitler – a page of drawings from Susan Miller's wartime sketchbook.

GERMAN AIRMEN
BALED OUT NEAR LOWESTOFT

S. MILLER

'German Airmen Bailing Out Near Lowestoft' – the moment captured by Susan Miller.

the school premises. Immediately, all classes were led quietly to the playing-fields. There we spent several hours waiting while the authorities came and searched everywhere. I am not sure that the girls were more disappointed than frightened when we were informed there was no bomb!

In spite of the raids and all the problems that were caused, in particular burst water mains, which necessitated supplying with fresh water – willingly carried out by our staff while the school was not functioning – there was never any question that we would continue our fire-watching duties, come what may. The spirit of Winston Churchill, now our Prime Minister, was infectious!

I was also a part-time ambulance driver during the war, based at No. 4 Surrey Street Depot. There I received instruction and carried out various duties. In October 1940 I obtained a certificate of proficiency in 'Incendiary Bomb Control', but I am thankful to say that the official crews adequately dealt with most of the troubles that subsequently came our way.

If I was ever in doubt that the powers that be thought an invasion by the Germans was possible, this was dispelled when we were given a typed sheet headed 'CONFIDENTIAL' and entitled 'Position and Duties of the Civil Defence Services in the Event of Invasion'. The first paragraph warned that the instructions, 'must not be communicated to any person outside the Civil Defence Casualty Service', and the text went on to instruct us how to pass on information we might discover of Military

'Sniper's Nest' – another contemporary sketch by Susan Miller.

'Ready For Invasion!' – a scaffold barrier and concrete blocks were erected near the home of Susan Miller.

my way was completely blocked by dozens of hosepipes and gaping holes and I had to give up. Eventually I tried to find my back to the depot in the blackness and was mightily glad of the assistance of a gentleman – whose face I never saw – who offered to guide me back. No headlights were allowed on vehicles then and the glimmer of light we had was no good for finding your way in places you did not know!

In one raid, when firebombs showered down, I went up onto the roof of the depot with the business end of a hosepipe. Down below a stalwart fellow manned the stirrup pump at full speed and we managed to put out several of the flaming bombs. It was only afterwards that I discovered that the water on the roof where I was standing had become electrified. How very wise it had been to wear rubber boots.

On another occasion, I had just received my full-length uniform overcoat. Suddenly the 'crash' warning wailed and everyone threw himself or herself flat on the ground where they stood. As I had only just put on my new coat, I stayed upright.

This reminds me of an incident when two friends and I were having tea in a very civilised way in our top-floor flat in the city. As we sat sipping our cups of tea, we heard the scream of a descending bomb. It must have been comical to see us gradually crouching lower and lower until only our eyes were

Importance, to deny resources to the enemy and how to react should the Germans occupy any local area. Above all else, the leaflet urged us, we must 'Stand Firm'.

Only once did I have to do my 'bit' – which turned out to be an abortive attempt. My assignment was to drive to the City Hall in pitch darkness. However,

The remnants of the invasion that never came: anti-tank trap near Ringland Bridge (above) and anti-invasion scaffolding on Brancaster beach (top).

above the table top in the hope we might see something! I recall that one such bomb caused a very bloody slaughter among girls fleeing from the works in Carrow Road.

It became our normal practice in the flat, almost every night when the siren wailed, to hastily put on something warm and rush downstairs – complete with the cat – and sleep on a neighbour's hearthrug until we heard the 'All Clear'. The cat, which was black and white, was named 'P.B.' (Partial Blackout), and once, while he was asleep in the sunshine on our tiny balcony, he rolled off. He fell three floors but still survived.

It was while I was walking between the Surrey Street Depot and home during that terrible April of the 'Baedecker Raids' that I had the idea of painting a series of pictures of the devastation the Germans had wrought on Norwich. Some of the scenes were almost surreal and certainly very painful. I am glad now that I painted them, as a record of a tragedy I hope will never occur again.

There was a great deal of 'make do and mend' necessary because of the shortages of equipment and materials. Our daily requirements were governed by food ration cards and clothing cards, which were not always of much use as the situation gradually became more acute, and so many things were in short supply. Rationing queues were an everyday sight in town and country, and people would get up before dawn to be ready for certain shops to open if it was thought they had fresh supplies of meat or fruit for sale.

In the craft department, various substitutes were inevitable: during lessons on patterns and printing, for example, sheets of paper and printing blocks were needed. In fact, satisfactory and attractive results were obtained by printing on advertisement pages of old newspapers, while scraps of card mounted on cotton reels took the place of lino or potato. I still have some of the girls' work with news of the war on the back.

Rushes gathered from the clumps growing on the

One of the curious steel turret anti-tank traps at Salthouse.

Above and below: *Hexagonal pillboxes strategically placed by the roadside at Oulton and Beccles.*

Disguised pillboxes. A coastal defence masquerading as a milk bar sketched by Susan Miller (top) and another in Bacton Wood intended to resemble a stable!

From top: *Guarding the beaches – pillboxes at Lowestoft, Corton and Yarmouth.*

local marshes could be braided, coiled and stitched in place of raffia. Intricate patterns on small pieces of material could be assembled to make costumes or bags. Norfolk reeds could also be cut as quills with which to practise manuscript writing.

Decorative bowls were made in papier maché using up odd pieces of coloured paper, and leather scraps were employed to create a portrait of the Madonna. Any ingenious idea was welcome – so we managed and got by. I also urged the girls to make up slogans and posters to keep up morale, and tried to inspire them with an idea of my own on the theme of 'waste not, want not'. The picture appealed, 'Do your Bit by Leaving no Bits – Prevention is Better than Cure.'

One of the strangest things of our 'war effort' at the school was tending the flowerbeds in the two quadrangles. They had been planted with hundreds of rose bushes, all bearing well. Each summer we undertook to cut all the full blooms down and take them to be dried in great heaps in the loft over the craft room. When the petals were dry and crackling like autumn leaves, they were packed in sacks and sent to a special centre where they were processed to supplement our medical supplies.

It was not quite so easy to supplement our food rations, and most of us were hungry a lot of the time. However, our supplies were, on the whole, adequate – but woe betide you if you lost your ration book!

A relic of the First World War at St Olaves.

The fate of a pillbox – collapsed onto the beach at Happisburgh.

'Pillbox on Kelling Heath' – a watercolour by Philippa Miller based on the remains of a pillbox and its spigot mortar base (opposite).

Some things were always hard to come by. My mother once said that she could only get one egg between autumn and Christmas.

My fellow teacher, Pamela Baker, and I often spent our summer evenings, when we were not on fire-watching duty or patrolling the school grounds during an alert, raising a few vegetables to supplement our meagre rations.

Occasionally, too, in the summer months, we were able to get away from the worries of wartime on our bicycles. Mounted up and fancy free, we spent a good deal of the time in the 'safe' areas on the lonely marshes and country lanes studying the wild life all around. We also sketched and occasionally fished for roach or perch using a branch, a length of cotton and a bent pin. A number of serious fishermen who sat for ages watching their sophisticated floats were actually not nearly so successful as us!

The marsh flowers in season were a delight, and marguerites in profusion were always a pleasure to me. But best of all, in those days of food shortage, was a fine bed of wild strawberries we stumbled upon one fine morning and left with our pockets full several hours later.

Occasionally, too, I was able to get away with friends to my little houseboat, the *Nutcracker*, still moored at Thorpe. Here we tried to forget our forebodings and our many duties and relax on the water. But even such pleasures could be brought to an unexpected end.

One summer morning two official-looking men appeared and asked if the boat belonged to me. When I replied that it did, one of them snapped, 'Well, you had better move it somewhere else or we will have to sink it!'

I understood the implication of what he was saying and asked where I could go. 'Anywhere outside the Norwich area,' was the reply. So I straight away began hunting and eventually found a suitable mooring in a dyke in Brundall, which enabled me to continue using the *Nutcracker* whenever I was free of duties.

The move turned out to be very successful in another way, too. Later, in order to escape the escalating air raids on the East Coast, my parents evacuated themselves to the same spot and lived on one of my father's cruisers, which he brought up from his yard.

When it was not possible to escape and sail on the Broads, Pamela and I found we needed something to do to keep ourselves awake during the long hours of fire-watching. So we decided to build a miniature house of the thirties. It might also be something to raise money for the war effort, we thought.

Pamela and I agreed the house should be one inch to the foot and made almost entirely from scraps and odds and ends – but complete in every detail. Apart from all the normal things, like tables, chairs, beds and furnishings, we vied with each other to produce the tiniest objects.

Wood was in short supply then, so the house had to be made from thick cardboard, with a thinner variety being used for the thousands of tiles on the roof. Eventually, after a year, the model was finished, even to the sink and bath taps, a lavatory that flushed drops of water, right down to a tiny box of matches in the kitchen. It had cost us just £1 for paint and electrical equipment.

There was also a mother and her little daughter who lived in the house, while the man of the family was serving in the RAF. For this reason we decided to call their home 'Spitfire Cottage'.

During the entire war, our little house only lost one tile, although some of the furnishing was temporarily in Coventry on the night of their famous 'Blitz'. By exhibiting our model residence to the staff and girls of Blythe School we managed to raise £40 towards the cost of building a new Spitfire for the war effort.

The amount may not sound much today, but we were assured in a letter from the Ministry of Aircraft Production, to whom the money was sent, that it was 'much appreciated'.

Before the war ended the 'Doodlebugs' [V1 Rockets] arrived over the Norfolk Broads. From a window of our flat facing east we could see the searchlights and tracer bullets as these flying bombs crossed the coast at Lowestoft. Anxiously we watched, because if their course was straight towards you, you were probably safe – they always turned aside before they descended.

I had one close encounter when Pamela and I were spending an evening on the *Nutcracker* at Brundall. Suddenly we heard the unmistakable sound of a Doodlebug going overhead. We cowered down in the boat, waiting fearful for it to fall. Moments later it did crash with an almighty crunch just beyond us in the direction of Norwich. As far as I know it did no harm.

At another time we were instructed in the ARP about the behaviour of the latest German weapon that was being launched at us – a small, anti-personnel bomb known as the 'Butterfly', though it

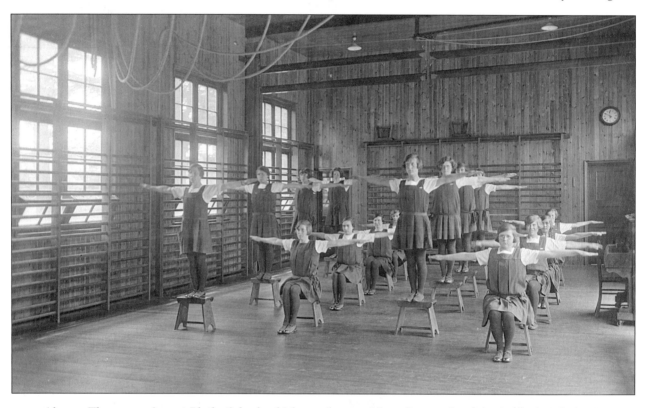

Above: *The gymnasium at Blythe School, which was destroyed by a German bomb in April 1942* (below).

Right: 'Do Your Bit By Leaving No Bits' - a 'make do' poster devised by Philippa Miller.

Top and above: *Ambulance crews at the Surrey Street Depot, Norwich.*

This page and opposite: *'Spitfire Cottage', created by Philippa Miller and her friend, Pamela Baker – exact down to the smallest detail. The model is now on display at the Stranger's Hall Museum in Norwich.*

*'Rationing' – a contemporary watercolour painting
by Philippa Miller, with typical food and
clothing cards.*

*One of a unique series of eyewitness illustrations painted by Philippa Miller in the aftermath of the
German raids on Norwich in April 1942: 'A Direct Hit in Grove Road'.*

'Remains of House in Oxford Street'.

'Ruins of Curls and St Stephen's Church'.

Another in the series of paintings by Philippa Miller: 'A.J. Caley's Chocolate Factory on Fire'.

Above: 'Peace Comes To The Norfolk Broads' - a highly individual celebration of the end of the Second World War painted by Philippa Miller in 1945.

Opposite: 'VE Day' – an evocative watercolour painting by Philippa Miller
of Norwich when the blackout finally came to an end.

had none of the beauty or grace of that lovely creature. They fell in clusters and were designed to catch on to any projection – a tree, a gutter, a telephone wire, a fence – and the next time they were shaken by a passing vehicle or even a person they would explode.

My memory of these weapons was of cycling while I was on duty and afraid that I might unexpectedly vibrate one that was hanging nearby. I made sure I kept to the dead centre of the road. Earlier we had taken part in a practice test in a wooded dell, where dozens of mock 'Butterflies' had been planted. We had to search for them and, as I found very few, this robbed me of any confidence I might have of avoiding them for real!

During the worst bombing raids, my friend Pamela, who lived on the west side of the city, along with her other duties, helped displaced families. She assisted them with their children, animals, rugs and packages on what was almost a nightly 'trek' into the country to find a safe and sheltered spot to sleep.

One of these families felt they were in luck one night when, despite the darkness, they found a convenient board by a field to camp beside. It was not until the next morning that they saw what was written on the other side of the board: 'BEWARE – UNEXPLODED BOMB'!

My last recollection of the war years in Norwich is quite different. Everyone remembers how the Americans arrived in East Anglia to fight alongside our forces in 1942. Quite a number of them liked to spend their off-duty hours in the villages of the Norfolk Broads, enjoying the scenery and the pubs. Most local people tried to make them feel welcome, as they were a long way from their homes.

A friend in Norwich told me how amused he had been when talking to one of the American airmen about the delights of the area. The red-blooded young man had apparently been very puzzled - my friend said - by the reference on a poster he had read inviting visitors like him to 'Enjoy the Norfolk Broads'.